GHOSTS OF AN ANCIENT CITY

Stories of Haunted York

by
John V. Mitchell

3rd Edition
1996

**Published by, and obtainable from
the Archives Department
St Peter's School
Clifton
York
YO30 6AB**

ISBN:

© **09529616 0 1**

© **St. Peter's School, York.**

Printed by York City Printers Ltd.
Unit 4, Birch Park, Huntington Road
YORK YO31 9BL.

ii

A Timely Warning

Reader, if timorous, thou hadst best
Give over here, and leave the rest
To such as feare not any evill,
And dares encounter with the devill;
To such as their dwellings have
By churchyards, or some noisome grave,
And lonely places, whose delights
Are to enter tombes, i' th' nights,
And charnell houses, who rejoice
To heere the screech owle's direful voice
And with earnest wishes longe
For the raven's boading song;
To such, or rather to more bold,
This my story must be told.
(From a poem written by a prisoner in York Castle, after the battle of Marston Moor
in 1644.)

Dedication

To the pupils of St Olave's and St Peter's Schools, York, who first badgered me into
telling some of these ancient tales.
　　　"Whilst yet a boy I sought for ghosts".
　　　　　　　　　　　　　　　　　　　　Shelley

Acknowledgements

Acknowledgments shown in the first two editions still stand for permission to use copyright material as follows:

Harrap & Co. "Masquerade" by Percy Hutchinson
Hutchinson, "Clifton Lodge", by Ethel, Lady Thompson
Souvenir Press, "More lives than one", by Jeffery Iverson

I have been encouraged by many people who wrote to me either with appreciative comments or giving their own experiences. The original witnesses of some of these strange events, Harry Martindale, Dennis and Rita Cole, and "Joan" have continued to tell their remarkable stories, neither adding to nor altering details over the years, and I am indebted to them.

Finally my deep sense of gratitude goes to Avril Pedley, Librarian of St Peter's School, for giving willingly her expert knowledge of modern technology in preparing this new edition for publication, and for all her help, hard work and encouragement.

Cover photographs by Fred Spencer.
Other illustrations taken from old prints of the city,
and grotesques from York Minster drawn by
John Brown,
late Art Master of St Peter's School.

Contents

INTRODUCTION TO THE THIRD EDITION

When this book first appeared 21 years ago it was produced to record strange happenings past and present that were part of York's heritage and traditions. As with national traditions such as King Arthur and Robin Hood, belief in the tales was left to the reader, the stories being part of folklore and memory and as such worthy of preservation.

I have never seen a ghost, nor do I expect to. I won't even say whether I believe in them or not, although I will continue to believe that something strange happened to Harry Martindale, Rita Cole and others who, though they didn't believe in ghosts and certainly weren't looking for them, nevertheless were willing to give me permission to use their experiences. They were ideal witnesses who had nothing to gain but might have lost a great deal by describing the events which took place. Their stories have not altered at all during the years.

These and other stories from my original research were first used publicly when Chris Martins, then Director of Tourism, asked me to arrange walks and talks for one week-end only to offer visitors a novel way of seeing York. We little imagined what this would lead to - talks on television and radio, countless articles in the journals of the world, and mention in many books on ghosts as "The Most Haunted City in Europe".

All this led to a ghost industry and several companies now offer nightly tours of haunted sites. "The Original Ghost Walk" still follows my original treatment without the need for gimmicks and bizarre effects. Although I have not been part of the ghost scene for many years, apart from giving talks in aid of charities and professional societies, I have had many requests to re-issue the first and fullest account which has not been available since the second edition. Here then, without frills or fantasies, are the original tales.

John V. Mitchell
Archivist
St Peter's School
York

The Barguest Legend

B elief in the barguest, a spectral hound of gigantic proportions, has long been part of popular superstition and folklore, and there are references to a barguest being seen on the walls, and in the castle of York.

Although the setting of the following account, in the Leeds Mercury Supplement of February 28th, 1881, is not York, it is at least Yorkshire, and the dialect is as interesting as the story.

"You see, sir", said Billy, "as how I'd been a-clock-dressing at Gerston [Grassington]. It war about eleven o'clock when I left, an' war at back end o' t' year; an' it war a grand neet. T' mooin war verra breet. I war passin' down t' mill, an' I heeard sommat cum past me, brush, brush, brush wi' chains rattlin' a' t' while; but I seed nowt; an' thowt I to mysen', now, this is a most mortal queer thing. Then I heeard again this brush, brush, brush wi' t' chains; for, yo' see, when I stuid still it stopp'd; an' then, thowt I, this mun be a Barguest, an' I hurried on toward t' wood brig, for they say as how a Barguest cannot cross watter; but, lord, sir, when I gat ow'r t' brig, I heeard this same thing again. An' then I becom' a valiant man, for I war a bit freeten'ed afore; an' thinks I, I'll turn an' hev a peep at this thing. So I turn'd back to gan hame, but I'd hardly reich'd t' door when I heeard again this brush, brush, brush, an' t' chains. I followe'd it, an' t' mooin then shone verra breet, an' I seed it tail! Then, thowt I, thou owd thing! I can say I've seen thee now, so I'll away hame. When I gat to t' door there war a girt thing like a sheep, but it war bigger, liggin' across t' threshold o' t' door, an' it war woolly like; an', says I, 'Git up', an' it wouldn't git up. Then, says I, 'Stir thysel'!' an' it wouldn't stir itsel'. An' I grew valiant, an' rais'd t' stick to baste it up, an' then it luiked at me.

An' sich oies [eyes]! They did glower! An' war as big as saucers, an' like a crewell'd ball; first there war a red ring, then a blue one, then a white one; an' these rings grew less an' less, till they come to a dot! Now, I war nane fear'd on it, tho' it grinned at me fearfully; an' I kept on sayin', 'Git up an' stir thysel';' an' t' wife heeard as how I war at t' door, an' she cum to oppen it, an' then this thing gatup an' walk'd off, for it war more fear'd o' t' wife than it war o' me! An' I call'd wife, an' she said it war t' Barguest, but ah've nivver seed it since; an' that's a true story."

The York Barguest

York also has its barguest, and stories of it were often told around the fire on winter nights. Sir John Reresby, the last governor of York, tells in his memoirs of a strange happening concerning one of his guards at the gate of Clifford's Tower in the year 1686. The night of March 7th was clear and moonlit, and, after the excitement of seeing a notorious witch tried and condemned, most of York citizens slept peacefully. About eleven o'clock, the sentry heard a great noise in the Castle and, going to the porch to investigate, he suddenly saw a scroll of paper creep from under the door, and turn first into the shape of a monkey, and then into a turkey cock. The soldier was surprised, we are told. He went into the prison and called the under-keeper who returned with him and also saw the scroll of paper dance up and down before once more creeping under the door. Was this the famous barguest? Sir John interviewed both men, but left the tale to be believed or not believed, just as the reader wished.

Perhaps the soldier knew of a curious poem which had been written in the year 1644 by William Paulden, a prisoner in the Castle, and a man called Wylkyns, who was in the service of Lord Fairfax. This is certainly not great poetry, but an extract is included here for its local interest, and for its information on the changing form of the barguest

"In Yorke the sixth day of October,
When I am sure the guard was sober,
Being farr distant from the day
When the soldiers had their pay,
About midnight when they saye
Greislye ghosts have leave to playe,
And dead menn's souls with coourage brave,
Skipp from out each severall grave,
And walke the roundes; when the bar-guest
Comes tumbling out of 's smoakye nest,
Sometimes having such a face
As promiseth an human race;
Sometimes he bee a beare, a dogg,
Sometimes the lykeness of a hogg!"

A Spirited Reply

Miss Simmonds and Miss Thorpe were not easily frightened; of that we can be certain. They owned a baby linen shop in Colliergate for many years, but were never as surprised as on the day they first opened it. It was an experience that was to remain firmly fixed in their minds, and they often spoke of it to their relatives, one of whom kindly passed it on to me.

Miss Florrie Thorpe, having spent a busy day organising and opening the shop, was tired but happy, and certainly had no thought of the supernatural. As she climbed the stairs to bed she saw the figure of an old man standing on the top landing, glaring down at her. She described him as being small and wearing a tail coat and tight breeches.

The most memorable thing about him was his expression. He was looking at her in absolute fury and hate. As she stopped half way up the narrow stairs, his face became even more contorted. "Get out!", he shouted, and put out his hands as though to push her downstairs.

Miss Florrie and her partner had often attended spiritualist meetings, so she was perhaps not as surprised as some people might have been. She showed her courage superbly, not only by standing her ground, but even answering the apparition back!

"I will NOT get out", she retorted. "This is my house now, not yours!" Whereupon the little old man looked surprised, as well he might, and disappeared - for ever.

Miss Florrie had the makings of a good detective. Fascinated by her experience, she began to make enquiries in the neighbourhood to see if there might be a possible explanation. She was right. Research showed that years ago a little old man, exactly like the one she had seen, had lived in the building when it was used only as a house. For some forgotten reason he had decided to live as a recluse, hating his neighbours and refusing all communication with the world outside. In particular he was careful never to let anyone cross the threshold into his house, and had a particular hatred of women. No wonder he had glared at Miss Thorpe.

But her courage did the trick. She was never troubled again, and the old misogynist had learnt his lesson.

Holy Trinity Church, Micklegate

It is appropriate that any tour of Haunted York should begin with this fine church, for it is the setting of what has become one of the most famous of all the ghost stories connected with the city. Ever since the Rev. S. Baring Gould, the writer of "Onward, Christian soldiers", first collected the many eye witness accounts in his book "Yorkshire Oddities", this particular haunting has always been included in ghostly guides to the north country. It is unique in that mention of it is even made on the church information board attached to the gate.

The church has been much altered since the time of the hauntings, although enough of the structure remains to enable us to imagine the scene when the gallery at the west end of the nave gave such a clear view of the phenomena at the east. It must be remembered, however, that the present east window is not the one about which the story is told, nor is it in the original position. The present chancel was built about 1886 on the site of the great central tower of the original priory church.

Three very distinct figures were seen, always in broad daylight, and generally during the hours of morning service. One of the figures, referred to as the mother, was tall and graceful, eighteen to twenty years of age, her face covered with a fine lace veil. This was the figure who showed such affection and despair. The second figure was described as a nursemaid, showing loving care of a child which she brings to the mother. Legend says that a father, mother and child lived near the church. When the father died, he was buried near the east window, but the child, dying later, had to be buried outside the city walls because of plague regulations. Soon afterwards the mother died and being buried in the husband's grave, "now, as in her lifetime, continues to seek for her child and bemoan the separation".

As has already been said, the building of the chancel seemed to bring an end to the appearances of these tragic figures. Perhaps the unquiet grave itself has been covered up, for there does not appear to have been any visual evidence of haunting since the 1890s, and the church is now quiet.

Yet, only in 1957, a strange incident occurred which was reported to me by a teacher of religious knowledge in a local school. This lady, during one of York's festivals, was showing a keen historian round some of the ancient churches of York. About nine o'clock in the evening, the two ladies came to Holy Trinity Church in the gathering dusk, neither of them knowing of the traditions of haunting connected with the building. As the historian examined the monuments and the fabric of the

4

building, her friend stood, somewhat tired, in the crossing at the west end of the church, underneath the place where the gallery used to be. Suddenly she noticed the atmosphere change to what she described as "earthy and cold, a very charnel house atmosphere of death and decay". It was not until 1964 that my informant heard of the tradition of haunting in the church and decided to visit the building once again. This time all was well, and the atmosphere was free of any unpleasant aromas.

Another tradition tells us that in the troubled days of Henry VIII, a party of soldiers, coming to take possession of the convent once attached to this community, met spirited reproval from the prioress, who barred the way and told them that only over her dead body would they enter God's property. Her courage resulted in her being cut down by their swords, though she vowed before dying that her spirit would haunt the site until what belonged to God was restored. Unfortunately the legend must remain unfounded, for the convent attached to the priory was St Clement's in Clementhorpe and we know that the last prioress was Isobel Warde who lived in a house in Trinity Lane, leaving it to the poor of the parish when she died. The house still stands in the narrow lane to the east of the church and is in use, with the delightful name of "Jacob's Well", for meetings.

Trinity Church, Micklegate.

All Saints' Church, Pavement

The tower of All Saints', Pavement, has long been one of the most graceful features of the city's skyline. By night the light, traditionally kept burning to guide travellers through the vanished Forest of Galtres, shows even more clearly the tracery and colour of its elegant design.

The church itself, even though much has been altered or has disappeared, still has many interesting features in its carvings, windows and ancient books. One important item from the past does seem to have vanished completely - the resident ghost. Although this figure never aroused the same interest and enthusiasm as the Holy Trinity ghosts, it was very well known, and was witnessed on many occasions. Unusually it always appeared during the day, and had a particular interest in funerals.

The figure was that of a woman, wearing a long white dress - or shroud. Her hair was described as being extremely long, but was always neatly dressed, in an attractive cluster of curls. Many people commented on her beauty, and her completely natural appearance, with clear complexion and cheeks glowing with health.

There appears to be no legend or tradition connected with her appearance. She seemed to have no purpose, no urgent message of reward or revenge, no real need to be there at all, except for her apparent urge to be present during funeral services. Is there a small clue in this?. Is she perhaps seeking some Christian way of burial that was once denied her? Is there here some relic of past tragedy of the kind which so haunted the imagination of Edgar Allan Poe - the premature burial? Many experiences have been recorded of apparent corpses reviving just in time to prevent burial, and there are even more nightmarish examples of bodies being found outside coffins when vaults have been re-opened for some later interment, their hands battered and torn in their frantic attempts to find some way out of their living tomb.

An experience of this kind is connected with the churchyard of St Saviour's Parish. It was once the custom to bury people with their personal jewellery, and a sexton of the parish, knowing that some valuable rings had been buried with a corpse, determined to have them. Coming by night to the graveyard he re-opened the vault, forced the lid from the coffin, and began to cut the rings from the body. But, in doing so, he cut the fingers of the apparent corpse. The lady was not dead, but had been buried in a coma, and the flow of fresh blood from her fingers awakened her, terrorising the rapacious sexton. So, to the delight of her friends, and the horror of the sexton, she was restored to her home and her friends.

6

But the ghost of All Saints' showed nothing of the distress that might have been expected following such a terrifying ordeal. She is reported only to have been friendly, especially towards an old market woman who once sold oatmeal in High Ousegate. This guardian of the ghost became the authority on the lady in white, and even claimed that she could call upon her to appear at any time. Unfortunately the death of the old oatmeal seller seemed to break the link, for the ghost also disappeared, leaving the mystery still unsolved.

All Saints, Pavement.

The Ghost of the Stairs

John Scrivener was not the man to believe in ghosts. He lived in a more scientific age at the turn of the century when rationalism had long since argued out the existence of such phenomena. It was not surprising, then, that he showed only polite interest when an old cleaning woman told him that she often had to leave her work undone in the evening, and go home, frightened to stay any longer in the old building by the river. It had once been the house of a prosperous merchant of York, but, like much of the property around it, had declined, and the peeling paint and dusty windows were sad indications of neglect and general decay. It was many years since the building had been a home, and much of it was used as offices for small firms who could not afford the rents of pleasanter situations.

One January evening, John Scrivener was walking in that direction when he met the old woman, trembling and horrified, as she stumbled as quickly as she could away from the house. He spoke to her, but could get very little sense out of her at first, except that she was able to gasp, "The thing is shrieking its life out in the attic." He quickly took her to her home, but had heard enough to rouse his full interest, and determined to return to the house to investigate the matter for himself.

He found the door still ajar, and by pushing it more fully open, he was able to see by the beam of a nearby lamp that the hall was quite empty. Lighting a small piece of candle in a battered holder, he climbed the stairs. The bare treads were steep and uncertain and twisted in many directions to serve the many levels and landings of the partitioned building. It was when he was about half way up that his heart thudded as he heard sudden screams from above, screams which were followed by strange muffled sounds as though regular blows were being struck with a heavy club.

His immediate thought was to bolt for the safety of the living world in the streets below, but he fought against his fear. He had come to investigate, and investigate he would. He felt in his pockets for matches, for he had no intention of being left in the dark by any sudden accident that might happen to the candle, and continued to climb the stairs, which at this level were even dustier and narrower than those below. When he reached the top landing he saw several low doors. The screaming and thudding had increased in volume, and he was able to trace the sounds to the door of a room which he knew must look over the river. He listened for a while, then with a sudden rush of courage, flung the door wide. The room was completely empty but the noise continued, and was obviously coming from a cupboard built into the far corner, where the ceiling lurched to meet the uneven floor.

He crossed the room, and opened the door, finding nothing more than a water tank. Of course, the mystery of the ghost was solved; those frightening screams were nothing more than the air being forced out of the pipes as water began once again to circulate after several days of frosty weather. As he watched he could see the ball of the cistern knocking against the sides of the tank, producing those dull regular thuds which had sounded so sinister. John smiled, relieved that he had solved the mystery, and delighted that he had found the courage to open the doors. It would be a comforting and amusing story to tell the old woman who had been so frightened for so long.

Yet, even as he turned to go, he heard a new sound, this time deep in the cellars; a dull, rumbling sound, as though a heavy load of bricks or coal had suddenly been thrown onto the flags and cobbles of the floor. At that very moment his candle flickered and died, leaving him in almost total darkness. Unnerved by this, he lit a match, but found nothing to alarm him. The small stub of the candle had burnt down into the socket, and the wick had fallen in, so that there was nothing for it but to strike further matches to see his way downstairs. He was just preparing to do this when he heard the sound of footsteps, slow, lumbering steps which began in the cellar, and then began to climb the stairs. The sound was uncertain and muffled, but was quite definitely the noise of footsteps with, between each footfall, a slight jingling noise like the rattle of a piece of lose metal.

Even though the sounds were slow, they came steadily on, climbing each flight until the top of the house was reached. John Scrivener, with every nerve and muscle strained, knew that by this time his courage had completely gone. He listened, scarcely daring to breathe, to the hesitation on the landing outside the room he was waiting in. He could see nothing, and was too terrified to strike another match, but somehow he knew that he was no longer alone. He could hear quite distinctly the slow tread of the footsteps and that curious jingling sound, and could guess from the direction of the   noise that the presence was crossing the room to the window overlooking the river. He turned his head, following the direction of the noise, for here there was a faint yellow light, but, as the footsteps stopped, there was no shape silhouetted against the grimy glass of the window, the house was once again utterly silent and he was alone.

Quickly he made his way out of the building, much puzzled by an experience that had completely changed his mind about the existence of ghosts. For a long time he searched to try to find some fact or legend which might account for the strange sounds he had heard, but without success. He never seems to have gone into the building again, and no doubt never expected to hear anything more of   the story. Yet this was not to be, for, a few years later, the decaying building was demolished. While they were working in the cellar, some workmen came across human remains, buried only a few feet under the stone slabs of the floor. Examination showed the bones to have been those of a powerful, heavily built man who had, near his feet, two rusty spurs, one of which was damaged, having a broken rowel which jangled as it moved.

Let the Dead Bury the Dead

Ghosts are no respecter of persons. Individuals who go looking for phantoms never seem to find them, yet ordinary folk, often uninterested in the supernatural, tend to find strange experiences when least expected. Such an event happened to Robert Johnson, a poor, uneducated man working for a butcher in Jubbergate.

He and a young assistant had been to a farm near Bishopthorpe to collect sheep for slaughter and were returning to York in the cool of a pleasant evening, driving the flock before them. The light was beginning to fail, so Robert was not pleased when the sheep stopped in a frightened wedge in the narrow lane, and the dogs, uttering thin whimpering cries, were turning away from them.

Angrily calling to the boy, Robert tried urging the animals forward, but none would move. Forcing his way through the terrified group, he joined his assistant and saw in the growing gloom the cause of the delay - a funeral ahead, the procession moving slowly along the lane. Robert could see the coffin borne aloft, presumably on the shoulders of the bearers. It had a costly-looking pall of black velvet and was followed by a clergyman whose head was bent over a prayer book. Obviously they couldn't be going far on that gritty road, thought Robert, and he was pleased when the procession turned towards a field.

He whistled to his dogs and, anxious to be home, urged the sheep on. But as he went he froze in a moment of astonished horror. He could still see the procession and now recognised the flowing robes as being those of a bishop. The coffin was dipping and swaying but as it moved more clearly into view, he could see that there were no bearers. The coffin was moving unsupported, five feet above ground, and even as Robert and his lad watched, coffin and bishop dissolved into the night air.

Somehow Robert Johnson and the apprentice struggled home with their sheep, and stammered out their experience to their neighbours. For a time it was the talk of the city but the butcher expected them to get over their shock in time. But it was not to be. Eventually the boy was released from his indentures, and took himself off to a less adventurous life at sea. Robert stayed on in his job but stubbornly refused ever again to drive sheep along the road from Bishopthorpe.

Robert was no scholar, so probably never realised that his strange experience might have been connected with an incident of history. On Monday, 8th June, 1405, Richard Scrope, Archbishop of York, was taken from his palace to execution in a field near Bishopthorpe. He had been accused of plotting to overthrow the Lancastrian king, Henry IV. Records state that he was carried face to tail on a broken down nag, and was wearing a loose blue robe with a hood. Seen in the fading daylight this may well have looked like a bishop's cope to Robert. Strange though that he was seen walking rather than on horseback. Perhaps at that stage of the journey the rough surface of the lane had caused him to dismount. One other detail rings true. The records comment that Richard Scrope prayed all the time for his executioners and those who had condemned him unjustly. Was this why Robert noted the "bishop" with his head bowed over a book?

Gateway to the Archbishop's Palace.

The Yorkshire Museum

The late caretaker of the Yorkshire Museum, George Thomas, was not the kind of man who would ever have expected to be in the news, for his was a life of the ordinary citizen of York, doing his work well, and relaxing with his family and his hobbies in his spare time. Nor was he a man with any particular interest in ghosts, though he was surrounded by the past. It is hardly surprising then that when he first saw the figure of a somewhat eccentric character, dressed in frock coat and drain pipe trousers, he thought it was one of the visitors or members who, busy in the Library, had not realised that it was time for closing. As he walked towards the figure, however, it disappeared.

This and subsequent sightings were to be the beginning of one of the most widely reported cases of haunting in York in recent years. It was also investigated in "Four Modern Ghosts" by Dingwall and Hall. The caretaker, obviously fearing ridicule, kept the incidents to himself, but, having seen some of the later phenomena, he mentioned the case to other people and gave them some idea of what was happening. A local doctor and a solicitor were among the first to be included in a small group of observers who decided to wait for the figure to reappear, but they were to be disappointed. Their vigil was rewarded however by the mysterious behaviour of a book which projected itself from the shelves and fell to the floor in such a way that it was impossible for anyone to have touched it.

There would seem also to have been some of the temperature disturbances often found in these conditions. The men were completely convinced that what they had seen was not due to the imagination of the caretaker, and experts were called in, but these later investigators saw and heard nothing, though again there were reports of the intense cold that had been reported before.

The book in question, a dull looking book called "Antiquities and Curiosities of the Church", had been presented by Alderman Edward Wooler, a solicitor from Darlington who had died many years before. Yet the description of the figure in the Library fitted him perfectly, and this was proved by a photograph of the alderman which was shown to the caretaker later. What was there about this book, we wonder, which made it so important to its original owner? He certainly seemed to be extremely anxious about it, moving along the shelves and muttering, "I must find it". The book itself is now in the City Library, and examination shows a rectangular brown stain on the inside cover, which looks as though some photograph or document had once been there. Perhaps this is what the ghostly alderman was seeking, but whatever it was has now gone, and with its disappearance there have been no reports of any disturbed presence in the quietness of the library.

Some time after these events the book was returned to the museum so that I could point it out in its original position to a party of journalists. On collecting the book after the weekend I asked if anything strange had happened. "Not really", I was told, "but on several occasions the museum alarm bells sounded, and continued until we removed the book from the shelves".

The Yorkshire Museum & Roman Multangular Tower.

The Theatre Royal

Theatres, like churches and pubs, seem to produce many ghost stories, and there are well authenticated stories attached to several London theatres. The Theatre Royal, York, has its own rival presentation which is probably the best known of all the York phantoms other than the ghosts of Holy Trinity. Most people have heard of the Grey Lady, but fewer seem to know that tradition gives another presence to the theatre, and possibly two.

The Grey Lady is one of those nebulous appearances so often connected with the remains of former abbeys, convents and priories. Ghostly monks and nuns are found in many classic cases of haunting, and the stone masons of medieval England must have enjoyed full time occupation walling up erring novices if all these traditions are to be believed.

The ruins haunted by York's Grey Lady are those of St Leonard's Hospital, the crypt of which now serves as a theatre club room and social centre. The hospital, with its many buildings, occupied a site of four acres, on land granted by William Rufus and King Stephen. Nothing now remains but the building near the library, which was probably once the ambulatory and infirmary of the original foundation, the crypt and some walls.

At some time during the long history of this hospital which was, incidentally, one of the first completely organised foundations purely for the reception of the sick and infirm, a young nun, whose name and life are completely unknown, is said to have been walled up alive. The traditional site of her ordeal is in the wall of a dressing room behind the dress circle. Originally approached by a spiral staircase, the room was very cramped, until recent alterations to the theatre.

Many occupants of this room mentioned the strange feeling they had of being watched while they prepared for their performances, and others noted that the room had a strange coolness which seemed to linger on. Actresses who were given this room often asked to change it for another without really knowing why, whilst others sat up all night in the hope of seeing the apparition. One member of the George Edwardes' musical company even dressed in the habit of a grey nun, appeared from behind a screen, and peered over the shoulder of one of the chorus girls busy with her makeup, a practical joke which went sadly wrong when the young lady screamed piercingly before fainting.

A more sympathetic approach was made by an Edwardian actress, the wife of Sir Frank Benson. Having heard the story of the tragic nun, Lady Benson spent the whole of one night in the old dressing room, praying for peace to come to the wandering soul. At the time this was thought to have put an end to the haunting, but strange happenings still occur, and a former actress, Mrs Marjorie Rowland, tells how, when standing at the back of the dress circle, she saw the figure of the little nun, dressed in grey with a white coif, leaning over the edge of the stage box.

The second ghost to be recorded is that of a leading actor in the theatre. Unfortunately no details of name or date are given, but the haunting seems to have been caused by an event in nearby Blake Street. A quarrel had given cause for offence, and a challenge was issued and accepted. The duel was fought in the afternoon, and the actor was killed. Yet that evening the company, having decided that the show must go on, was horrified to see their former leading man staggering about in the wings. Perhaps he objected to his understudy's performance!

The Grey Lady

The famous Grey Lady of the Theatre has certainly not disappeared with the passage of time. Since the first publication of this book she has been seen on several occasions, by local residents and visiting companies alike. The tradition is now firmly fixed that her appearance heralds a successful production. She was included in a 1981 broadcast on haunted Theatres of England, where the ever vigilant Frank, stage door keeper and a dedicated researcher into the story of the Grey Lady was interviewed. Sadly he still hasn't seen her, which is surprising for he probably spent more time alone in the theatre than anyone else. Perhaps she likes company in every sense of the word for, in the same broadcast, two actresses told of their experience of the ghost of the theatre. During an on stage rehearsal of "Dear Octopus" the assembled company, including Miss Evelyn Laye, saw a strange misty figure at the back of the dress circle and were convinced that the Grey Lady was watching their rehearsal with great interest.

Even more recently a small group of researchers were able to gain further psychic information on the lady. Interestingly enough the traditional story of the nun who was guilty of an illicit love affair did not emerge. Far from having been walled up, this young lady, who gave her name as Therese, had merely been imprisoned in her cell for claiming to have seen angels at mass. She had been harshly treated, and ordered by the sisters to remain there or she would be punished even more severely, for she had a "black and lying tongue".

Two gifted sensitives were present, and with the help of a kindly priest, a very private and extremely moving ceremony was held in which the little nun was given spiritual consolation, release and absolution. Now she may rest in peace, but this does not necessarily mean the end of the Grey Lady story. Her soul may now rest, but a certain historic "thought-form" may still be apparent from time to time, just as a photograph of a loved but departed friend may still be seen and treasured.

The Middlethorpe Mystery

Not far from the present Middlethorpe Hall, on the road from Bishopthorpe to York, there once stood an Elizabethan manor house, of which all trace has long since disappeared, together with all records of the family which once owned it. It was a house "of baronial dimensions" and it must certainly have been of unusual size for it held, like Glamis Castle, a particular secret which could be known only to the head of the family, being passed on to the heir just before the death of the owner.

The last holder of the secret, a woman whose name we do not know, became suddenly ill and died before she was able to hand on the necessary information to the next in line. When this lady was buried, the coffin was taken through a gap made specially in the wall of the estate, the hole afterwards being filled in. (This curious custom is found in many parts of the world, and is designed to prevent any wandering soul finding its way back into the house.)

Drawn by J. P. Neale.   Engraved by Radclyffe

BISHOPTHORPE PALACE,
YORKSHIRE.
The Seal of the Archbishop of York

London. Published by Jones & Cº Janʸ 10. 1829.

Several nights after the funeral, a member of the family was awakened by the sound of quick footsteps and a sobbing, moaning cry. He imagined that one of the servants, returning late, had been locked out and was in some distress, so, disregarding the fact that it was already midnight, he got out of bed to look through the window.

It was a clear, cold night, with only an occasional cloud to dim the light of the almost full moon. He could see clearly the figure of a lady on the other side of the wall. Her hair was worn long, and hung over her white dress, and with a sudden sense of horror he recognised the face of his recently departed relative. To and fro she went, as if seeking a way in, her face anguished and despairing. The sight proved too much for him, and without attempting to speak to her, he rapidly returned to his bed.

After this first appearance the ghost was regularly seen by many people living in the district. Always she showed the same anguish and frenzied attempts to find her way into the house, but unfortunately no-one ever summoned up sufficient courage to speak to her.

Eventually the terror caused by the dead to the living proved to be too much for the inhabitants of the house. It was deserted, and later demolished. Curiosity cannot be satisfied, for nothing whatever was found which could in any way explain the secret, or the reason why that wandering soul seemed so anxious to impart its information. Whatever it was, the disappearance of the house ended the unhappy vigil of its former owner and must have brought peace to her soul, for she was never seen again.

A Medieval Mystery

One of the great classics of ghostly literature is M.R. James's "Ghost stories of an Antiquary". In addition to writing these, Dr James, who was Dean of Durham and Provost of Eton, had a wide interest in the whole subject of hauntings generally. Whilst researching in the British Museum he came across a twelfth century edition of Cicero, on the blank pages of which an unknown monk of Byland Abbey had written down, probably about the year 1400, a series of ghostly happenings from his own neighbourhood.

One of these concerns the ghost of Robert de Boltby who had died and been buried in his local churchyard, but who had a habit of leaving his grave by night and wandering through the streets, standing by doors and windows of houses as though he were waiting for someone to help him. Dogs followed him, barking loudly and, not surprisingly, the peace of the village was disturbed.

Some young men determined to catch him if they could and came to the cemetery, but when they saw him their courage deserted them and they fled - all except two. One of these seized the ghost (how he managed this we are not told) and put him on the kirkstile, saying that he would hold him fast whilst his companion ran for the village priest.

Along came the cleric, and, in the name of the Holy Trinity, commanded the ghost to speak. This it did, not with its tongue but "inside its bowels as it were in an empty cask". Good solid Yorkshire ghost this, with none of the classical twitterings and squeakings of Homer's ghosts.

The spirit made its confession, that it had been an accessory to murder amongst other things, and the priest gave it absolution, commanding the two men who held it never to reveal what it had said. "And, henceforth as God willed, he rested in peace."

Not a very exciting story it is true, but it has been included to show how little the details of hauntings have changed. It is all very familiar: the churchyard, the disturbed dogs, the false courage of the young men (and their hasty departure), and, eventually, the quiet ending.

The Ghostly Funeral

Elliott O'Donnell in his book "Haunted Churches", published by Quality Press Ltd in 1939, mentions these stories, and also adds another fascinating tale connected with St Crux church. Some years previously he had been told of a policeman passing the church late one night who was surprised to hear the sound of the Funeral March being played on the organ, in crescendo. It was startling to think of a funeral service being carried out at that time of night, particularly when there was no sign of hearse or funeral carriages. Gradually the music began to soften, and the door of the church slowly opened. The astounded policeman, watching intently, saw nothing, but he was conscious of something coming out of the church, for not only did he hear the rustling of dresses, but also felt them swish against his legs as they swept by him.

When this ghostly procession ceased, the door of the church gently closed, and darkness and silence once again surrounded the church. It is an interesting parallel to the experience of Harry Martindale (*see* Treasurer's House) that the policeman concerned was reported to be a very matter-of-fact and non-imaginative person.

In the same book, Elliott O'Donnell also records the sighting of a female figure in a shroud coming out of the church and following the musicians either down Fossgate, vanishing as soon as it reached Foss Bridge, or along Colliergate and St Andrewgate, disappearing suddenly as it reached Spen Lane. It is difficult to decide whether or not this is yet another ghost of St Crux, or is in fact a variation of the female figure who followed the York Waits long ago (*see* Waiting at the Church).

He also seems to have made use of Camidge's book (although he calls him P.J. Camidge) for he mentions the strange apparition of a phantom rabbit seen scampering about the aisles of St George's Church at night, or in the early hours of the morning. Attempts to catch it have always proved unsuccessful. This apparition has also been reported to be that of a large white cat, and, for some strange reason, is supposed to be the ghost of Dick Turpin buried in the old cemetery of the church.

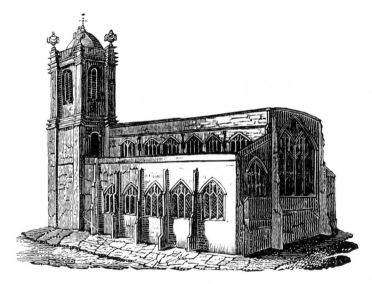

St. Crux, Shambles.

Blood Sacrifice

When Richard the Lion Heart was king, and crusading spirit ran high, there was living in York a small but wealthy Jewish community. Two of its leaders, Benedict and Jocenus, travelled to London for the coronation of the king but, in a rising storm of anti-Jewish feeling, were attacked so severely that Benedict died of his injuries on his return to York. On March 19th, 1190, a disastrous fire broke out in York, and under cover of this Benedict's house was looted and his wife and family murdered.

Jocenus had his house in Coney Street, on the site where the premises of Messrs Leak & Thorp were until recently. Sensing trouble, he was given permission by the Constable of York Castle to take his wife, his wealth and his compatriots to the castle for safety. Inflamed by the oratory of a white-robed monk, crying, "The enemies of Christ must be destroyed", the mob attacked the walls of the castle, the monk himself being killed when a dislodged stone dashed his brains out.

Clifford's Tower in its original state.

The Jews then offered large sums of money for their safety, but these were rejected by the maddened rioters, so, following the advice of their rabbi, the Jews decided to kill themselves rather than fall into the hands of their Christian adversaries. Their goods and treasures were heaped up and set ablaze and, amidst the smoke and flames each man cut the throats of his wife and children before being killed himself. Lastly Jocenus had his throat cut by the old rabbi who, surrounded now by the bleeding bodies of his compatriots and the terrified members of the group who had been too afraid to kill themselves, died proudly.

The survivors of this terrible event, hoping in vain for mercy once they had opened the gates, were massacred by the mob, nearly fifteen hundred people perishing in the few days of the riots. For many years after this it was noted that the stones of the castle would suddenly appear stained with a deep red. Scientists held that this was because of the action of a certain fungus on the limestone of the walls, but the older inhabitants of York knew better - it was always "Jews' Blood".

Although not strictly within the meaning of the words "Ghost Story", recent experiments in regression hypnosis therapy by Mr Arnall Bloxham of Bristol produced material which does form a link with the above story. BBC Television produced an absorbing documentary film, "The Bloxham Tapes", regarding the work of this acknowledged expert, and his experiments were also written about in "More Lives than One" by Jeffrey Iverson, published by Souvenir Press in 1976, a most interesting book generally, though only two of its chapters deal specifically with York.

I have heard the Bloxham tapes, and in one of them Arnall Bloxham's subject, now in her forties, was hypnotised and as the personality Rebecca gave a description of a busy though not particularly happy life as Jewess living in York in 1189. She gave details of the family, and her large stone house to the north of the city. She describes the clothing, adding the fact that Jews had to wear yellow circles over their hearts to show their nationality. She records rising tension because of anti-Jewish feeling, and the fact that many of the citizens were heavily in debt to the Jewish community; her account seems to mirror the national feeling leading up to the Third Crusade. Names were given which suggest some of the documented characters of the period. She mentions, for example, a man called Mabelise, who must surely be Malebisse, described by a medieval chronicler, "Richard, rightly called Mala Bestica", or "evil beast" (a name which, incidentally, survives in the place name of the nearby village of Acaster Malbis).

In dramatic detail, Rebecca tells how, hearing screams and smelling smoke from the house next door belonging to Benedict who had died of the wounds he received in London. In a very agitated manner she tells how her family fled, her husband and son carrying their money in sacks on their backs. They fled to the castle by a back way, gaining some precious moments by deliberately throwing down some of their silver to delay the pursuing mob.

Eventually they reached the castle, but seem to have been allowed only within the outer walls at first. Later they seem to have reached what they thought was the safety of the keep, but even then they could hear the mob screaming and shouting outside, and the ominous sounds of the ramming of the gates. It was then that the tragic killing of the children by their own parents began.

Yet somehow, and Rebecca suggests that someone who had been paid to help them got them out, she, her wounded husband and her two children reached the sanctuary of a church "outside the big copper gate of York". Her husband and son left the church in search of food, leaving Rebecca in a state of further agitation and hysteria as she saw the flames and heard the horses coming. The mob entered the church screaming, "Burn the Jews" and rushed down to find Rebecca and her daughter Rachel. The recording ends with the agonised cries of Rebecca as they take her daughter from her and then the ominous words, "Dark ... dark".

When the tape was splayed to Professor Barrie Dobson, Reader in History at the University of York, and the acknowledged expert on the massacre of the Jews, he found the story, apart from some discrepancies of language and topography, "impressively accurate". It was strange, however, that Rebecca had not given in her story the best known historical facts, namely the growing tragedy in the castle itself. In addition to the appalling scene on Friday, 16th March when the men cut the throats of their wives and children and then killed each other, other Jews lost their lives when, having made a huge bonfire of their possessions, they were persuaded to come out on the promise that their lives would be spared if they accepted Christian baptism. This promise was false, and, amidst the flames which had spread from the bonfire to the wooden walls of the castle, the survivors of that terrible night were slaughtered.

One feature of Rebecca's story that did not, at first, seem accurate was her assertion that she and her family had found refuge in the cellar of a church. There were originally over forty churches in York but the snag was that, with the exception of the Minster, not one of them had the necessary crypt in which Rebecca claimed that they had hidden. This did seem a definite drawback until, in September 1975, after the tapes had been recorded and studied, a chance discovery by a workman in the development of the medieval church of St Mary in Castlegate as the setting for the York Story exhibition brought remarkable evidence. Something was discovered that does seem to have been a crypt, and the presence of stone arches, vaults, Roman and Anglo-Saxon masonry makes it very clear that there was a church on that site, a church with a lower level. Was this chance discovery of the twentieth century a direct link with a traumatic life and death in York of the twelfth century?

An intriguing story for further details of which I can strongly recommend the reading of Jeffrey Iveson's book. Not only is the Rebecca story given in full, but there is also a detailed and intriguing story of what the subject claims was her life as Livonia, the wife of a tutor employed in the household of a Roman named Constantius living in a villa on the outskirts of "Eboracum" as York was then known - fascinating reading for the historian as well as for the student of the unusual.

St. Mary, Castlegate.

Blood is their Argument

In 1385 York was seething with activity and crowded by troops and mercenaries. The building of the Minster choir, begun twenty-four years earlier, was reaching its final stages, Archbishop Alexander de Neville having presented a hundred marks towards the building fund, in addition to a pair of gold and silver plated candelabra. Perhaps he needed to ease his conscience, for he had shown more interest in enlarging and fortifying his castle at Cawood than in furthering the work begun by Archbishop Thoresby. Already de Neville had made many enemies by his overbearing and turbulent manner. He had quarrelled violently with his own clergy on church matters, and with the Mayor of Hull on the right of wine tasting in the port. The mayor, less patient perhaps than the priests, snatched the archbishop's crozier out of his hand and belaboured several of His Grace's attendants with it and for this had been brought before the court. In 1388 this quick tempered and violent archbishop surrendered his office and was banished.

It was a time of quarrel and high tempers generally, with jealousy, turbulence and ambition leading towards the eventual deposition and death of the king himself, in mysterious circumstances at Pontefract not many years later. But at the time we are thinking of Richard II was visiting York to make preparations for an expedition against the Scots, and was staying, together with his retinue, as a guest of the archbishop at Bishopthorpe.

Details of what followed are obscure, but it seems that the king's half-brother, Sir John Holland, hearing that his servant had been killed by an arrow, rushed out to avenge the death. He met Lord Ralph Stafford, who was entirely innocent of the brawl, and struck him. This led to a duel, which was fought in a field near the palace, and Stafford was killed. Sir John fled to Beverley Minster to claim sanctuary and was eventually dispossessed and banished, being later pardoned on the intervention of John of Gaunt, Duke of Lancaster.

For many years after the event, the road leading past the scene of the tragedy was haunted by the ghost of the unfortunate Ralph Stafford. Many people who saw him testified that he was tall, and strode purposefully along, whilst others, seeing him more closely and clearly, noticed that the figure showed blood from a wound just above the heart. These death wounds often appear in cases of traditional haunting, being apparently used either as signs of recognition of the departed, or in an attempt to win sympathy from the onlooker, though a blood-stained spectre is likely to create feelings of horror rather than pity in most people!

The Duel

In the long history of the city violent deaths were a regular feature, and executions, murders, massacres and warfare must have added many spectral figures to the city streets. To this list must also be added death by duelling, for many such deaths there must have been, even though we have details of only a few.

One that we do know about has, however, produced a ghost. On the morning of Sunday, June 11th, 1797, two officers in the 46th Regiment of Foot, stationed at York, fought a duel on the banks of the river at Fulford. We do not know the cause of the quarrel between Mr George Crigan, surgeon to the regiment, and Lieutenant-Colonel Bryan Bell, but we do know that the surgeon was killed, and the colonel, with his two seconds, was arrested and imprisoned in York Castle.

At the subsequent murder trial the evidence given to the jury must have persuaded them that this was an affair of honour, and that there must have been some justification for the challenge. For this reason the murder charge was reduced to that of manslaughter, and the officer, instead of a trip to the three-legged mare of York, was sentenced merely to a month in the city gaol on Ouse Bridge and a fine of 6/8d.

Obviously the small value set on his life annoyed the defunct surgeon even further, for he showed his displeasure by "stalking about" the scene of the duel for many years afterwards, an unusual but efficient method of complaining about the vagaries of English law. He now seems, however, to have received some satisfaction in a higher court and has disappeared completely from the banks of the Ouse. Or is it perhaps that the field he stalked for so long now bears a heavier burden of cars and concrete?

The Ghosts of York Minster

A book published in the middle part of the last century tells of a strange happening in the Minster. Originally the full names of the people concerned were given, but these were later suppressed to avoid distress to the family. Mr B.L. had taken some friends to see the Minster, and, as the party was numerous, it had divided into small groups, Mr B.L. himself being with a gentleman and his two daughters, some distance away from the rest of their friends. As they turned away from a monument they had been interested in, Mr B.L. saw an officer in full naval uniform coming towards them. He was surprised to see anyone so far from the sea wearing uniform, and, pointing out the stranger to the elder of the two ladies, he was astonished to see an immediate paleness and signs of considerable agitation in her face, which increased as the figure became more distinct in the gloom of the cathedral.

Thinking her to have been taken ill, Mr B.L. called for her sister to come to help them, but by now the figure in naval uniform was directly in front of them. The lady gazed at it, breathing heavily and showing painful intensity of feeling. The form was now close to them, and, approaching the lady, whispered in a low and scarcely audible voice, "There is a future state." It then moved on to the aisle of the Minster.

The lady's father now arrived to assist his daughter and, leaving her in his care, Mr B.L. hurried after the mysterious visitor. He searched on every side but could see nothing and, although he listened carefully, no sound of retreating footsteps could be heard on the echoing pavements of the cathedral.

Baffled in his attempt to discover the man whose presence had so disturbed their peaceful visit, Mr B.L. rejoined his companions. The lady asked her companions to continue their tour of the building, assuring them that she would be perfectly all right with her friend. This they agreed to, and as soon as they had gone she begged him not to mention the reason for her agitation.

She explained that she wished to protect her father from the sorrow which was to come to him, and also that she wouldn't be believed in any case. "For", she said, "I have seen the spirit and heard the voice of a brother who no longer exists; he has perished at sea." It appears that she and her brother, wishing to clear or confirm religious doubts which they both had, once made a pact that whichever of them died first, should, if possible, appear to the other.

And so it turned out. In due time news arrived to verify the presence seen in the cathedral, and it was discovered that the brother had died on the very day and hour that he had been seen by his sister and Mr B.L. in the north side of York Minster.

There could also be another ghosts in York Minster, as shown by a visitor to one of the cathedral concerts during the Festival who complained afterwards that his enjoyment of the music had been spoilt by a monk walking up and down the aisle. The Scottish visitor was even more disturbed when he discovered that people sitting in the aisle had seen nothing all evening.

Then too there is the tantalising story of a possible ghost seen in broad daylight by a visiting school teacher with a large party of children. At first the figure, that of a man dressed in a white Elizabethan costume, had been assumed to be a person in fancy dress. When this case was reported to me I also assumed that there was a natural explanation, particularly as I knew that a performance of a Shakespearean play was being given that week in the grounds of Grey's Court. So I did not investigate, and the school party returned home. It wasn't until some time later that I discovered that the play had certainly been held on that particular day - but in modern dress! Yet another ghost who got away.

The South=West View of York Cathedral.

The Five Sisters Window

Although this is not strictly a ghost story, the following incident is included here because it deserves recording in more permanent form than the correspondence column of a newspaper. On November 30th, 1933, The Times printed a letter which Mrs Helen Drage Little, widow of Colonel Charles Blakeway Little, C.M.G, had left to be sent to the editor only after her death, which had occurred on November 8th of that year.

In the letter she explained that, having seem the first trainloads of wounded arriving from Gallipoli, and witnessed the untiring devotion of the nurses, she determined that after the war a memorial should be erected to the women who had made the supreme sacrifice, yet might have been forgotten.

On November 30th, 1922, she had the following visionary dream. She appeared to be in York Minster, going to evensong, and had entered by the south transept door as usual. As she reached the choir door she saw two figures in white in the middle of the north transept, one beckoning her and the other pointing to the Five Sisters Window. Moving towards them, she recognised her two sisters, both of whom had died as children. As she looked up, she saw the great window move slowly backwards like a door, revealing a garden full of strange yet beautiful flowers. Under a great tree in the middle of the garden, five women sat weaving whilst, over a small river, came a number of girls and women, wearing misty grey-blue garments. They came nearer and nearer, when the window suddenly swung back, hiding the beautiful scene.

After this experience she determined to restore "The Five Sisters Window for the Sisters", and within nine weeks over 32,000 subscribers had raised more than enough. The window was unveiled by the Duchess of York, the present Queen Mother, on June 24th, 1925.

In connection with this restoration it is interesting to know of a link with an earlier building of ecclesiastical Yorkshire. At the dissolution of the monasteries. the lead was stripped from the roof of Rievaulx, melted down and moulded into long bars called "pigs", each stamped with the Tudor rose of the new owner, Henry VIII. These were stacked tidily in the nave but, before they could be carted away, the stone vaulting of the roof fell in and covered them completely. There they stayed, and there they were found four hundred years later, during the excavations by the Ministry of Works, who, on hearing that the Minster needed lead for restoration work, presented them to the Dean and Chapter for use in the Five Sisters Window.

The Witness

Before the present building in Lendal known as the Judges' Lodging was used for that purpose, there stood at the beginning of Spurriergate a large Elizabethan mansion. This timber fronted house had originally been the town house of a rich merchant family called Appleyard, two of whom were Lord Mayors in the middle of the sixteenth century. After the family had left the house it was, for a time, used to accommodate judges during the assizes. The house itself, standing opposite what was then Jubbergate, but is now Market Street, probably occupied the area where Woolworths now stands. It has long since disappeared, although Robert Davies, in a public lecture on December 19th, 1854, stated that he could well remember the building. It was this place that Charles Dickens used for a story he told in 1879 in a magazine called "Leisure Hour".

One bitterly cold November night in the early part of the nineteenth century, two lawyers arrived in the city to attend the winter assizes. They were given lodgings in the "ancient, timbered and dark building". One of the men, having stayed there on previous occasions, knew the house well, but the accommodation he was shown to, a large room on the second floor, was strange to him. He was told that the ceiling of the room he usually occupied had fallen in, and this alternative, though hastily prepared, looked comfortable enough in the light of candles and a flickering fire.

Both travellers were weary, and one was suffering from a heavy cold, so, after a meal downstairs, they each went off to bed where, drowsily appreciative of the warmth of the fire, they were soon asleep. The time was eleven o'clock.

At two o'clock one of them awoke and felt unaccountably afraid. The fire had gone out, and the room was in complete darkness. He sat up and was feeling for a candle and tinder box when suddenly he heard a noise, a muffled, slippered sound of someone walking away from the bed. Almost immediately this was followed by a voice crying, "Henry! Henry!" which seemed to come from downstairs, followed by an agitated argument, fast and fierce. Sounds of a scuffle followed, then a shriek and a heavy fall.

The lawyer, too terrified to strike a light, now waited tensely in the dark, his alarm considerably increased by the sound of someone climbing the stairs, stumbling heavily. It was a slurred, uneven sound, as though some injured person were dragging his feet heavily along.

The sound grew louder in the passage, drawing nearer and nearer. The lawyer longed to cry for help, but his tongue seemed paralysed as the steps reached the door. He waited, and still they came on till he realised in a sudden rush of terror that they were now inside his room, even though there had been no sound of the door opening or closing. There came a gurgling cry, the sound of a heavy fall, then all was still.

The remainder of the night was spent in terror and semi-consciousness, and the next he knew daylight was breaking, and a maid, bringing hot water, was knocking. He called out for her to come in, but her insistent knocking at last forced him to get out of bed to open the door for her. It was only then that he made the unnerving discovery that the door was firmly bolted - on the inside.

As soon as he dressed, the lawyer told the housekeeper of his experience. Somewhat shamefacedly she explained to him that what he told her was no new thing, for others had also sensed the same terror and distress, and for this reason the room was hardly ever used.

She gave him the following story by way of explanation. More than a century before, a judge, said to be of a sullen disposition, was staying in the house with his young nephew, heir to a large fortune. One night the occupants of the house heard strange sounds from the second floor, and in the morning the servants discovered the young man dead on the floor of that particular room, with stab wounds in his chest. Because of the judge's position the matter was hushed up, and a verdict of suicide was brought in at the inquest.

Slender facts, which leave room for wild but vain speculation. The house, with its ghost, has long since gone, and no trace of the story has ever been found in official records, but it would seem that the ghostly sounds gave a truer account of the tragedy than the inquest verdict.

T' Dog Knows

The doyen of the Minster policemen in the last century was old Gladin. He was a most prosaic and unimaginative old man, quite incapable of making up or imagining a ghost story, and yet he had a strange and inexplicable experience in the year 1879.

He always took his dog with him when he was on night duty, generally without incident, but one winter night, as he and his dog were sitting on a bench in the nave of the Minster, the dog suddenly jumped up and bolted in the direction of the north transept. Gladin got up to follow it, fully expecting that someone was hiding in the darkness of the building. As he crossed, his attention was caught by a curious apparition under the north-west tower.

It was a shaft of blue light, about the height of a man, which passed slowly to the centre of the great west door before gliding up the centre aisle. Nothing daunted, Gladin followed the apparition and saw it crossing to the south transept. Here, in the east corner, the strange light remained for at least ten minutes before flickering away, apparently through the stones in the wall.

Gladin, strangely puzzled, went to look for his dog. He found it cowering by the door, whimpering and shivering in abject terror, and as soon as he opened the door it bolted, and could never again be persuaded to enter the Minster. If Gladin whistled for it and tried to get it to follow him, it would look wistfully at its master, and then slink off with its tail between its legs. Some people suggested that this strange experience was all a dream, but whenever this theory was put to him, old Gladin would chuckle and say, "Well that mun ask t' dog. T' dog knaws!

Headless Hauntings

Even though nothing quite as spectacular as the ghost of Anne Boleyn "with 'er 'ead tucked underneath 'er arm" can be claimed for the city, whether it is animal or human head which is missing, Yorkshire can produce quite a number of topless terrors.

During the eighteenth century, a woman living alone near Bishopthorpe was thought to be very wealthy, and for this reason was murdered one autumn night by someone unknown. The murderer hid her corpse in long grass which grew under a clump of trees near her home.

Weeks passed before the body was discovered, and by that time, because of decomposition, her head had become separated from the rest of her body. Coffined and cared for at last, the corpse was buried in the churchyard of St Andrew, but this was not to be her resting place. Nightly, near her grave, or by the clump of trees where her body was found, the woman walked. She always appeared headless, and wrapped in a shroud, wandering to and fro as though seeking something - her lost treasure perhaps, or her murderer - or maybe her missing head!

She was seen mostly near the clump of trees on the towing-path between Middlethorpe and Bishopthorpe. Often, she waited underneath one particular tree, disappearing quickly if anyone tried to approach her, but remaining in full view of any who showed signs of fear. Reports of the ghost of this unlucky lady lasted until the end of the Victorian period when, like her cottage and the clump of trees, she finally disappeared.

The Cantering Cavalier

Strong emotions often produce lasting effects on the atmosphere, as can be seen in many of the haunted battlefields, so it is hardly surprising that traditions of ghosts apparently connected with the Battle of Marston Moor should persist until the present day. Stories are told of the many ghosts who appear on the site of the battle, and of blood-stained soldiers galloping through the lanes of the district.

Most famous of all these was said to be the appearance of a headless figure. As soon as the village clock a mile or two away chimed the hour of midnight, the phantom would rise from the ground. He was on horseback, and was wearing the type of clothing which could only be afforded by an officer. He seemed to pause for a while, as if in deep thought, then, with lightning speed, he galloped along the lane for a mile or two.

Suddenly halting, he waited again as if in search of some scene or action. Then forcing his horse once more into a gallop, he rushed still further, travelling a considerable distance before quietly returning. His search was always in vain, and, like a weary and dispirited hunter, he returned to the place of his original appearance, and sank slowly into the ground.

Perhaps his appearance is connected with the experience of two men who were driving from Filey to Harrogate on Monday, November 5th, 1932. They were crossing Marston Moor when they ran into fog, almost too thick for car lights to penetrate.

At that same moment, a motor coach arrived behind the car, and, by the extra light, some men were seen wearing long cloaks, top boots and large turned-up hats with cockades. The driver of the car watched them closely so as to prevent any collision, but, when the car passed the figures and he turned his dipped headlights fully on, the walkers had disappeared.

He got out of his car with his passenger, angry with the men in cloaks for blocking the way, but the road was completely empty. There was no place for anyone to hide, only a grass verge by the side of the road, and hedges too high to leap over and too thick to scramble through.

Several years ago I was talking to a historian of the area. He told me that once, when he was visiting the scene of the battle, he saw on a small hill a group of figures in the costume of the battle period. There were three or four men, all looking excitedly round them. Thinking that some film or enactment of the battle was in progress and not wanting to intrude, he crossed the field as quickly as possible, but, on turning round, the area was completely empty, nor was there any place where the figures could have hidden. Perhaps the officers of the Sealed Knot have more recruits than they are aware of whenever they re-enact the action of the Battle of Marston Moor.

The Stolen Head

A third headless ghost traditionally haunts the churchyard of Holy Trinity, Goodramgate, although there are very few details of its appearance. The parish registers do record the burial of Roger Layton, executed in 1469, and this may account for the spectre. Another theory suggests that the presence might be that of the Earl of Northumberland who attempted to put Mary, Queen of Scots, on the throne of England. For this he was brought to York, convicted of treason, and, on August 22nd, 1572, beheaded on a scaffold set up in Pavement. Many people looked on him as a martyr, soaked handkerchiefs in his blood, and gathered up the straw of the scaffold. His body was buried in the church of St Crux by two of his servants and three women, but his head was set on a very high pole on the top of Micklegate Bar. Here it remained for some time until, as James Torr records in his book, "1574 ... the Earl of Northumberland's head stolen in the night from Micklegate Barr by persons unknown". It has been suggested that some pious Catholics, the persons unknown, gave the head Christian burial in Holy Trinity, and it is this that causes the appearance of the ghost.

That the disappearance of the head was the work of some pious Catholic sympathiser seems likely. Even as it lay in the Tolbooth on Ouse Bridge, waiting to be stuck on a pike for display at Micklegate Bar, a saddler, William Tesimond, living in the parish of St Michael-le-Belfry, cut some of the hairs off the beard and wrapped them in a paper on which he wrote, "The hair of the beard of the good Earl of Northumberland". Later he was brought before the High Commission to explain his words, and his precious relic was confiscated. He was probably the father of Oswald Tesimond who was at St Peter's School with Guy Fawkes and the two Wright brothers, John and Christopher, all of whom were to be implicated in the Gunpowder Plot. Oswald became a priest and spent some years with the famous Jesuit, Father Edward Oldcorne, who was also educated at St Peter's. Arrested after the Gunpowder Plot, he was racked five times whilst in the Tower of London, on one occasion for seven hours, yet revealed nothing. He was eventually executed near Worcester on April 7th, 1606 and has recently been beatified.

Holy Trinity, Goodramgate.

The last heads to be spiked on top of Micklegate Bar were those of the unfortunate Jacobites beheaded after the Battle of Culloden in 1746. Twenty-two rebels were executed on Knavesmire, most of whom were buried behind the Castle walls, but strict instructions from the Government ordered that the heads of William Conolly and James Mayne should be set up on the Bar. The traditional position was on each side of the central stone warrior on high spiked poles set in iron sockets. T.P. Cooper records that the original poles lasted until the end of the nineteenth century when they were chopped up for firewood by a tenant of the Bar chambers.

The heads of the Jacobites remained until January 1754, when, under cover of a snowy night, they were stealthily removed. The Lord Mayor was informed immediately the theft was discovered, and a proclamation was issued offering a reward of ten pounds for information leading to the detection of the offenders. The Government, concerned by this reappearance of Jacobite sympathy in the north, sent an urgent letter to the City, demanding to know what action had been taken, and the reward was increased to £112.10s. Great excitement followed when a journeyman cooper called Thomas Wake, whilst in a cobbler's shop near the Bar, pointed to the turrets and claimed that he was the man who had taken down the rebels' heads. He was arrested and brought to trial, but it was soon discovered that he was guilty only of the dramatic boastings of a drunkard.

Eventually, an unknown Irish journeyman, tempted by the high reward and the promise of a free pardon, revealed that he had assisted his master, William Arundell, a Roman Catholic tailor of York, to carry away the heads for reasons of faith and chivalry. At the Lent Assizes in 1755 Arundell was sentenced to two years' imprisonment, fined £5 and ordered to pay £200 sureties for his good behaviour for two years or more.

One last word as to the economics of dealing with traitors. In 1557 it was agreed that the following item should be paid out of the corporate funds:

"the expenses of boiling, and carving, and setting up the carcasses of the late traitors, about this city, amounting to 12s 6d." This, at least, is one charge that present day rate payers cannot complain about.

A Ghostly Guardian

In 1975, after the original publication of this book, I heard of a remarkable experience from a lady visitor to the city - an informative, amusing and fascinating correspondence followed.

The lady, who prefers to remain anonymous, was in York for a few days in connection with genealogical and historical research. Although she had an interest in ghosts and some experience of psychic happenings, she tells me that on this occasion her interest in the City was purely historical and architectural. She had been in York for only two hours, and was exploring on foot. The weather was rather chilly and overcast as she walked over Ouse Bridge and along Micklegate. She approached Micklegate Bar with particular interest - examining its upper structure carefully, and musing on the fact that, after the Battle of Boroughbridge in 1322, the severed heads of several connections of her family, a name extremely well known in English history, were exposed on the Bar.

Suddenly, as she walked onto the walls proper, glancing down at the bank and the moat, she felt an extraordinary change come over her. She was about four metres from the Bar when she was assailed by acute terror, and an icy feeling around the solar plexus. Despite being in London throughout the blitz and being under fire during the war, and although as an investigator she had been in some very haunted situations, never had she experienced such a manifestation of menace as she did on that June afternoon. She pressed herself against the wall, and looked towards Lendal, thinking how far off it seemed, and knowing quite clearly that she just couldn't return to the street through Micklegate Bar. Strangely enough there was no other person visible on the wall to whom she could turn.

Micklegate Bar, with the Barbican.

Then, as she looked down at the parapet, she saw the lower half of a male figure. He was wearing brown leather sandals, and above his ankles she noticed the fine gold hairs of his legs. His sandals and gown were similar to those worn by a Franciscan friar, though the few inches of the homespun gown she saw were black rather than the brown she might have expected. Then came, quite clearly, a firm male voice saying, "Don't be afraid. Follow me!" Gratefully murmuring "Thank God", she followed the feet along the centre of the parapet with great confidence until, after a few metres, the figure disappeared.

Obviously from the colour of his gown her rescuer was a Dominican, a black friar of the community to whom a church was given in 1228 by King Henry III. This church, dedicated to St Mary Magdalene, was the burial place of Lord Mowbray, whose remains had hung in chains since the Battle of Boroughbridge. This might suggest that the Dominicans acted in charity for the prisoners condemned to death. It is tempting to wonder whether or not this remarkable experience took place because of the relationship of the lady to some unfortunate ancestor whose head had been exposed.

It is also interesting to speculate why only the feet and lower legs could be seen, although in some detail. My informant has herself suggested that had she perhaps been more psychic she would have seen not only the rest of the friar, but also the unknown assailants who were causing her feelings of terror.

Waiting at the Church

At the end of the Shambles, in Pavement, stood the large church of St Crux, demolished in 1887. Remains of the church have been built into the present parish room backing onto Whip-ma-whop-ma-gate. Whether the transferred relics include the two ghosts once associated with the church we do not know.

The first one, a tall, bold-looking man, was often seen standing by one of the windows, looking intently into the street. This ghost was unusual because it always seemed to appear in the very early hours of the morning, so that it became a familiar sight to the women of York going to their cleaning jobs before the rest of the city was astir. The women often called out to him, but he would never appear outside the church, nor could the women ever be tempted to venture inside the building to investigate.

The second ghost of St Crux was a great lover of music. She was always on hand to welcome the Waits of York, four or five men who, splendid in scarlet livery

The old street of Pavement, with St Crux Church on the right

and silver badges, were given £4 a year to play during the winter months and act as combined watchmen, weather forecasters and speaking clocks. The ghost, a beautiful figure in white we are told, always came out of the churchyard as they passed, following the group at a short distance, and stopping wherever they did. She listened intently to their playing, moving along with them, but always at a respectful distance. At first she alarmed one or two of the performers, but eventually her frequent appearances caused them to look for her, and to call out to her, but without reply.

Along Colliergate they went, into King's Square, and then, just as they turned into Goodramgate, she disappeared as suddenly as she had arrived.

Two Women

Just over a hundred years ago, according to Camidge, most streets of York had their own particular ghost, and many stories could be told. It is unfortunate that he didn't record more of them, but he has given us two very contrasting cases.

In what he described as "a very quiet street in the centre of the city" (later research suggests that this was St Saviourgate), once stood a large, old-fashioned but comfortable mansion which, for a whole generation, remained empty, its forlorn and deserted appearance giving rise to the belief that it was haunted.

According to tradition, just as midnight sounded from the church tower, a beautiful lady would appear. She had long, flowing hair, a fine figure and an appearance of gentility. She appeared at the door of the house, walked past the churchyard, then stood at the end of the church as though waiting for someone. To and fro she walked until, as the clock struck one, she returned to the old house.

In spite of her gentle aspect such was the terror caused by her regular visits that no-one would live in the house and, over the years, it grew dirtier and drearier until eventually it was demolished and on its site the present Lady Hewley's Hospital was built in 1840.

The second lady ghost was far from gracious. She lived in a house in Coppergate, opposite the west end of All Saints, Pavement. Camidge describes her as a modern ghost, explaining that she was dishonest, mean and wicked. Although she was tall and handsome her dishonourable business life had aroused the hatred of all who knew her.

As she lay dying, her room is said to have echoed to strange noises, and her bed was surrounded by unearthly visitors. She died at midnight, in a small, badly-lit room, screaming protests against death, cursing and announcing her intention of coming back.

And so it was, tied to earth by her own greed and thoughtlessness, she remained in her old house, making her presence known by unearthly noises similar to those heard at her death bed, and for many years no-one dared use the room in which she died in case they should be made too forcibly aware of her continued presence.

The Back Seat Driver

It is surprising that no-one in the Victorian era ever thought of making a play about this particular story, as it has all the necessary ingredients for a successful melodrama - wronged country maiden, caddish villain, faithful swain, and affecting death scene - and, eventually, a ghost!

In the days when highwaymen were busy on the roads of England, there lived in Sheriff Hutton a farmer's daughter whose name is given only as Nance, who was engaged to a boy called Tom. Not long before their wedding, however, a gaudily dressed stranger appeared, who soon flattered Nance into eloping with him, promising her a life of ease, wealth and luxury in which she foolishly believed.

39

Tom, heartbroken at this desertion, gave up his farm work and became the driver of a coach making regular journeys between York and Hull. One day about a year after he had begun his new job, he was some five miles from York when he noticed sitting beside the roadside a young woman nursing a baby. With a sudden thrill of recognition he saw that it was Nance, but sadly altered, and obviously exhausted. She was able to tell Tom how, since leaving her village, she had been cruelly tricked and neglected. Her fine gentleman turned out to be a rogue and a highwayman who soon deserted her and her child, and she had since discovered that he was already married.

Moved by her plight, and still much in love with her, Tom helped her into the coach and continued his journey to York, making arrangements for her to be looked after by kindly Mrs Pulleyn at the York Tavern. But, in spite of all care, Nance was too weak to recover. Before she died, she begged forgiveness for the hurt she had caused him, and asked that, if ever he had loved her, he would care for her child and bring it up as if it were his own. In return she promised that, if such a thing were possible, her spirit would watch over him and guard him and his children from all dangers.

Tom was never to see her again - or so he thought - and probably had almost forgotten about her promise. About two years after her death, however, a remarkable happening was to bring the whole incident back to his mind. He was in Durham, and had collected four important gentlemen who were most anxious to be in York by a certain time, promising him four guineas if they arrived safely before 8.00 p.m. Tom had every confidence in his driving ability and knew that arrangements had been made to change horses at every stage.

All went well until the last stage ten miles from York, when the driver of a post-chaise travelling northward gave Tom the unwelcome news that thick fog was spreading from the city, and was worsening every minute. Before three miles had been covered, Tom's spirits sank. The fog grew denser and denser, and although he knew the road well, it would obviously mean creeping along at a very slow pace if safety was to be maintained. Just as he was reining in the leading horses a slight figure appeared out of the curling mist. Lightly she sprang to his side and laid her hands on the reins. At once the leaders broke into a gallop and regained their former speed, the coach swaying alarmingly to the terror of the passengers who yelled for him to slow down.

On and on they went, the guard sounding his long coach horn as a warning to other traffic on the road. On and on, through the fog which was now so dense that it was impossible to see more than a yard in front. Yet Tom, smiling to himself, was not afraid. Against his hands he could feel colder yet gentler fingers guiding the reins, and he knew who sat beside him.

40

On lurched the coach with nothing to be seen, and it was only the rattle of the wheels on cobbles that told Tom that York had been reached. The comforting touch of those fingers disappeared. A few minutes later Tom reined in his foam flecked horses at the sign of the Black Swan in Coney Street. There were five minutes to spare before the appointed hour, and Tom had earned his four guineas. "Poor Nance, poor Nance", he was heard to say as he walked away.

This was not the only time he was to be helped by his former sweetheart, and, when the time came for him to hand over his business to his children and grandchildren, Nance obviously decided to continue her protection. She appeared one bright moonlit night so suddenly in front of a coach travelling from Pickering that the horses reared and damaged the coach springs, which meant a return to the forge near the Black Horse Inn in Yorkersgate, Malton. This delay seemed unfortunate at the time, yet was one which prevented the coach from being held up further along the road to York by three masked men who had been lying in wait for it.

As Old Tom said, "If Nance comes to your help, let her have her way; think on, if she signals you to stop, then stop. If ever she takes the reins, let her drive." He knew that Nance was paying her debt.

The Black Swan, Coney Street, 1820

41

The King's Manor

One of the most historic buildings of York surely deserves its share of ghosts, and, if traditions are to be believed, this former abbot's house, royal dwelling, fashionable seminary for young ladies and one time assembly rooms, has several lingering presences from other days.

When the building was the Yorkshire School for the Blind I lived there for almost three years, and was lucky enough to be given stories and traditions of its ghosts by a lady who had lived and worked there for many years.

She told me of the black cowled figure of a monk still occasionally seen about the buildings, a relic of the time when the central stone house belonged to the Abbot of St Mary's. Another story said that in the stone flagged passage leading from the inner courtyard to the old bowling green, groans still linger from the Roundhead dead and dying who were laid there after the unsuccessful attack on the Manor on Trinity Sunday, 1644.

Then, from a teacher came two other strange incidents. For a period of some weeks she was awakened every morning at 2.50 by a strange sound exactly like the cracking of a whip. It is well known that floorboards in old houses creak, but surely not at the same hour or over so long a period. The other incident concerned a cupboard in the wall. Although the door of this cupboard was always firmly closed, it often swung open, but only when a particular scarf was hanging in it and, strangely enough for a building with royal connections, the scarf was of a Royal Stuart tartan.

Another story concerned the newest wing of the building, added as a Principal's House by a York architect, Walter Brierley, in 1900. The ground floor of the building was being used as sick quarters for the children when I was there. One afternoon a maid scrubbing the floors screamed, and was discovered in a fainting condition. On regaining consciousness she was very distressed, but eventually she was able to explain that the cause of her fright had been a lady who had come out of a cupboard and walked straight through her! Small wonder that she screamed. She described the appearance of the lady, who was wearing a green dress and carrying a bunch of ribbons. The gown, from the details she gave, seemed to be of a Tudor design.

The maid saw the figure again on several occasions, its visits always occurring in the afternoon. As her fright grew less, the girl was able to see that the apparition was holding not, as she first thought, a bunch of ribbons, but a bunch of roses.

The wife of a member of staff decided to keep watch with the girl. At the usual time the maid cried out, "There she is. Can't you see her?" Unfortunately the staff member could not, but she did hear a rustle and a swishing sound as of a very full skirted dress passing her.

The maid left and returned to Ireland, and no-one else ever saw the lady in green. But the mystery remained. It seemed strange that the girl was able to give such a detailed account of Tudor costume when her interests were anything but historical. It was odd, too, that the figure should haunt the newest part of the building. Yet the story, with its attention to small details such as the bunch of roses which she at first thought were ribbons, seemed to have truth behind it. But, with the departure of the only person who saw the apparition, interest waned, and it was only some time later that another detail was added to the story. I discovered in a local bookshop a history of the building. This contained a manuscript plan which had been made before the building of the new wing, and there, at right angles to the north west side of the forecourt, appeared a long rectangle labelled "Former Rose Garden".

The Manor House Porch.

Recent reports have been made of the difficulties in keeping a portrait hanging on the walls of one of the upstairs rooms, a portrait of a gentleman in Stuart costume. This may well have a link with an earlier incident. Some years before the war there were reports that the ghost of a Stuart nobleman had been seen. One Hallowe'en, four teachers at the school decided to watch out for him. Wisely they had agreed that whatever they saw they would say nothing, but would each go to their own rooms, write down their experiences, and compare notes the following day.

Late on October 31st they began their vigil in a corner of one of the old rooms of the Manor. The particular room they chose had two doorways. One led from the staff rooms and the other, used by the children, had an archway and a flight of stone steps leading downwards into the room.

All was quiet until, about midnight, they all saw a figure coming slowly down the stone steps. Because of the decorated arch and the steepness of the stairs it appeared only gradually. They first saw buckled shoes, then the lower legs, then silk breeches and, finally, a doublet or jacket.

It was at this precise moment that further identification proved impossible for the door behind them was flung open, and the headmaster, who had only just heard of the experiment, angrily entered and sent them all to bed, forbidding any further research into the subject. His wrath was obviously too much for the ghost as well for, with his appearance, it vanished abruptly.

The Haunted Ballroom

Ghosts can suddenly appear in the most unlikely places. Most people, asked for a setting for a ghost story, would choose a ruined abbey, a crumbling castle, or a gaunt mansion mouldering in some deserted place. But recently ghostly activity has been reported in cinemas, aircraft hangars, modern council houses, hotels and even supermarkets. Yet, so far as I know, there has been no other example of a haunted ballroom.

Bishophill has been for generations a place crowded with the living and the dead (and, probably, the living dead as well). In this area there are several haunted sites, houses and churches mostly, and the setting of this modern city ghost is in a building, once ecclesiastical, but now adapted for use during the week as a school of dancing, expertly run by Mr and Mrs Dennis Cole.

It was as a result of a newspaper article in February, 1969, that I first received details of this case, and heard the experience of five reliable witnesses. Mrs Cole often heard curious sounds of money being counted. The noise resembled that

St. Mary, Bishophill=the=Younger.

of a church collection being emptied onto a table, the coins being "slipped" into a box (with the noise becoming louder all the time) until eventually, with the sound of a metal box being shut, there was silence once more.

Leading from the floor of the building into the hall itself is a long, low corridor with tiled floors. Frequently Mrs Cole heard the sound of quick, light footsteps approaching the hall, but, although the steps reached the door, no-one ever entered.

Double doors leading from the hall into the churchyard and always securely locked, began to rattle and move so violently that daylight was visible under them as they moved backwards and forwards, and the door handle was seen to turn. This happened on two occasions when private lessons were being given. One man, realising that there was no wind to account for this movement, stood on a chair to look through the small panes of glass over the door, but no-one was there.

More remarkable events were to occur whilst Mr and Mrs Cole were on holiday. Another teacher of the school was left in charge, a man ideal for the purpose of independent witness in that he had been inclined to scoff at earlier reports of abnormal activities. After classes had finished one night, he returned from locking the doors to the main hall. At one end of this is a small platform on which

45

stand chairs and record players. There is also a small wall shelf holding various books on the technique of dancing.

As he looked he saw one of these books sliding horizontally from its usual place. For a yard or two it moved in mid-air, before coming down with a very heavy thump, as though it had been thrown with some force. The sight was too much for him. Although not easily scared, he rushed out of the hall, slamming the door behind him, but forgetting to lock it, so that the police, on their rounds, had to call Mrs Cole's mother (Mrs Marshall) to check that all was well inside the hall.

Mrs Marshall also was able to report strange occurrences. At the back of the hall are several small rooms leading to the coal cellar and an outside door. One morning she was in the cellar when all at once the atmosphere changed. There was an oppressive mustiness about the place, and, not liking this, Mrs Marshall turned to go. Suddenly she was pushed in the back with such violence that she was sent sprawling up the steps.

In the centre of the hall itself is a net suspended several feet from the floor. This is used to hold balloons for special festivities. On one occasion when several people were in the hall, though no-one was actually on the dance floor, a discarded cigarette packet quite suddenly sprang into the net, without anyone being near it.

A visit to the hall was arranged by a small group of investigators but on this occasion proved uneventful, apart from a "cold spot" in the centre of the floor which gave a reading of 3° Centigrade, the specially sensitised thermometer dropping steadily from the surrounding 8°. Tests were made to discover physical reasons for this such as draughts from doors or the presence of water underneath the floor, but nothing was found which could account for it.

The other strange thing was that recording equipment could not be made to work. First an electric socket failed, then the motor of one recorder jammed, and finally a microphone could not be made to function properly. A telephone call was made for an expert to come, bringing with him a new, tested microphone. This he did - and it didn't work either! Strangely enough, five years later when the Nationwide television crew were filming in the hall, exactly the same thing happened. The leading sound technician said that his recorder had been switched off, which astonished him, as it had never happened before and meant the re-filming of the whole sequence.

Included among the group who investigated the phenomena one February afternoon was a gifted sensitive who prefers to be known only as Marjorie. She was able to use her gifts to good effect, and correctly described the presence responsible for much of the activity. Various corroborative details were given, all of which were recognised by Mrs Cole and, for a time, the strange happenings ceased.

But, strangely, Mrs Cole missed her ghostly visitor, who for many months gave no indication of its presence. Visitors came and went, yet, apart from the failure of electrical equipment and visiting journalists, no activity was reported. Until, unaccountably, strange things began to happen again, though never with the same force as the original phenomena. Once more the footsteps were heard along the corridor, not only by Mrs Cole but by pupils having afternoon dancing lessons. Two nurses in particular, who had previously been somewhat sceptical, had good cause to remember the time when they were convinced that some invisible presence had entered the hall. In the festive atmosphere of a Christmas Eve dance, Mrs Cole was sprinkled with water from an unknown source, and a large and expensive bottle of perfume crashed to the floor from the centre of a table, without any damage to the fragile glass. The Coles's dog on more than one occasion showed unease, bristling and growling at an unseen presence which it followed round the room.

During a lull in the dancing, two young girls were startled when a hairbrush which one had put on an empty chair next to her, suddenly rose into the air before falling to the ground and, whilst she and her friend were looking at it, exactly the same thing happened to a tenpenny piece on the empty chair at the other side of the children.

A couple who were new to the area and knowing nothing of the strange happenings in the hall were also made very aware of the inexplicable. Following an afternoon lesson they were leaving the hall when, in the corridor, they met a woman coming in. The wife was very conscious of the long and hard stare given to her and, when they reached the outer door, commented to her husband that she wondered why the woman coming in had stared at her so much. "What woman?" came the reply.

"Why, the one who passed us in the corridor just now."

"But there was no-one in the corridor." It was then that the puzzled wife realised that her experience had been stranger than she had at first realised.

Coming back to the dancing class that evening, she mentioned the fact to Mrs Cole who, without mentioning anything of the earlier stories, asked her if she would be able to recognise the lady again. On being assured that she could, having been able to describe the person thoroughly, she was then shown a group photograph from a formal banquet, and she was able to point to a figure and say, There she is, there's no doubt about that." No doubt indeed, but, seemingly, yet another strange incident in the story of the dancing school, for the lady in the photograph was a well-known dancing teacher, a lady with a vibrant personality and a deep love of the dancing school, and a lady who once said to Rita Cole that she would never leave that building, the same lady whose funeral Rita and Dennis had attended several years previously.

Suffer, Little Children

The small street of Bedern was once a square. Here stood a house which, since 1575, had been used for the reception of old and infirm people, who were granted pensions of about a shilling a week by the city. In 1847 the old people were moved and the building continued in use as the York Industrial Ragged School. One particular workhouse master was of a ferocious and cruel temperament, and, under his doubtful care, several children are said to have died. Their ghosts, three of four of them, appeared not only to him, but to passers-by. They appeared especially at midnight, to play in the street, to the amusement of those who saw them. But the master of the institute, like Queen Victoria, was not amused, for strange noises and appearances occurred, especially around a cupboard where it was said the victims of his neglect and cruelty were kept until he found opportunity to bury them. Indeed, when the poorhouse was being moved to the bottom of Marygate in 1855, it was reported that several more bodies were discovered, and nervous people long afterwards refused to enter Bedern after dark, declaring that ghosts still appeared, to the great terror of beadledom. Well, he deserved it!

This traditional ghost story was taken originally from William Camidge's book and, in first adding it to the list of York ghost stories, I decided that, like so many others, it was a thing of the past. It would seem, though, that I was wrong. Recent demolitions and excavations have altered the appearance of Bedern, and the Victorian building erected on the site of the former Ragged School has itself disappeared, leaving a clear view now of the old Dining Hall of the Vicars Choral. It has often been the case that alterations seem to start off ghostly activity, and the Bedern site now seems to be included in this.

On one of the conducted ghost tours of the city a local resident on the outskirts of the group listened very intently to the story of the ghostly children of Bedern. At the end of the evening he approached the guide and told him how much he had enjoyed the evening, and the story, for it seemed to throw some light on a strange experience of his own. Apparently he was in the habit of taking his dog for a late night walk along Goodramgate, and one moonlit night he was passing the entrance to Bedern when he heard the sound of children's voices. Wondering why youngsters should be about so late, for it was nearing midnight, he turned under the archway. To his great surprise his dog, who normally would not leave him, growled and bristled under the arch, and could not be persuaded in any way to accompany its master, so that he had to leave it where it was and continue on his own. As he came out of the other side of the archway the sound of children at play stopped and, search

Old houses in Bedern

as he might, he could find no trace of any human activity on that clear moonlit night. It was interesting too that before joining the group he knew nothing of the tradition of haunted Bedern.

An archaeologist working on the site also had unusual experiences. He reported a feeling of being watched intently and, as he bent over his trowel, he constantly felt someone tapping him on the shoulder as though to attract his attention but, when he turned round, there was never anyone near. Naturally a disbeliever in ghosts he laughingly mentioned the occurrence to his wife. Nothing more was thought of this until that night, as he was preparing for bed, when his wife noticed on his back several red marks - scratches almost - running from the shoulder downwards, spaced almost like the prints of tiny fingers.

The city has several buildings that were once used as orphanages and poorhouses, and the sight of grey and blue coated charity children must have been very familiar to the citizens of York. One of these buildings, modernised and altered beyond the belief of its former inmates, is still used for the welfare of children but in a very different way. Yet there still seems to be a link with its former history. In the corridors of the building footsteps have been heard, and a mist-like figure has been seen on the stairs at times when the building has been completely unoccupied apart from the maintenance staff.

The footsteps and the figure have been heard and seen by several people concerned with administrative work, and seem to be those of a woman. On one occasion a lady working late heard someone coming into the office next door, crossing the floor, and then the noise of drawers being pulled out as though someone was searching for something. Yet the room was completely empty. Letters and documents in desk drawers and filing cabinets have been moved in a way that cannot be explained by carelessness or wind movement. A significant feature of this phenomenon is the fact that the only papers ever to have been disturbed are those dealing with the adoption of children.

One of the houses in Precentor's Court was the scene of a curious incident concerning a child ghost which was never fully explained. One dark winter night a young lady decided to visit some friends whom she had not seen for some time. The house she called at was in darkness but, thinking that her friends might be in a back room, she knocked. In fact she knocked for some considerable time before a door was opened and she saw the figure of a small child which shone with an unearthly light. Quickly this light grew until it filled the whole doorway.

Terrified, the young lady ran to some other friends living fifty or sixty yards away and told her story. Some of the men, shaken by her obvious alarm, went to investigate but found nothing. The house was completely dark and the front door firmly locked, as indeed it should have been, as the occupiers had been away for over a month.

Some time ago I spent a most interesting morning with Mrs A.K.H. Fletcher who gave me, in a most charming and convincing manner, details of strange happenings in and around York, stories concerning her own experiences as well as those of her relations.

An old house has stood very close to the Minster for hundreds of years, and holds within its walls the remains of a great tragedy. People living in the house were often aware of a sadness which filled the rooms, and of the sound of a child crying in the upper part of the house. So distinct was this that a nanny, now an old lady, would often go upstairs, thinking one of her babies was in trouble. The two children living in the house were also well aware of it and, as they grew older, one of them once said, "Don't let the little girl come in and sit on my bed tonight, 'cos I don't like her crying all the time." Nanny, hearing this, realised that the situation was most unsuitable for the children to be in, especially when the two girls began to talk so frequently of the strange visitor. She also knew it was not imagination, as she herself had seen the figure - a little girl in an old fashioned white dress. The children were given another room, and the small room with a window overlooking the Minster became a spare bedroom. But even so, guest were unable to sleep peacefully, being disturbed by crying and the sound of little feet running along the passages in a tense and desperate manner.

So troubled did the family become that eventually they arranged a seance to discover more about their pathetic visitor. Through the medium they were able to discover the little girl's name, which has, unfortunately, now been forgotten. She was able to tell them that she had died of starvation in that house in an outbreak of plague which occurred in the seventeenth century.

The city records state that 3,512 citizens of York died, and so severe was the pestilence that the Minster and the area round it was "close shut up all this year". Amongst the victims were the parents of the little girl and, knowing this, and believing that the child also had died, the servants fled in terror and the house was deserted. But the girl recovered and her terror and distress can well be imagined. Alone in the house, with the bodies of her parents, and no-one to help her. Poor lonely child - small wonder that she still looked for comfort from later inhabitants of the house.

Another sad figure from the past was once seen in St Olave's church by Mrs Peggy Atkinson, an aunt of Mrs Fletcher, who used the church regularly for many years and was herself very interested in psychic matters. She always sat in the back pew of the church and one morning she saw in front of her two people whom

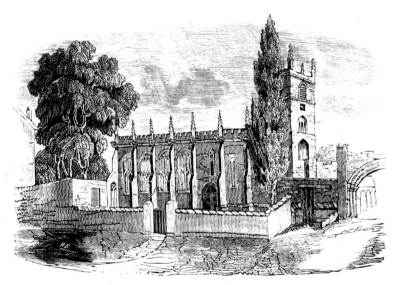

St. Olave, Marygate.

51

she did not recognise - a woman, and a small boy aged about ten. She became interested in them for the woman was in deep mourning, and so was the boy. The style of their clothes intrigued her, and she thought it extraordinary that some people should still possess clothes of such an outdated fashion. The boy was wearing a dark grey Norfolk jacket, and the woman with him appeared to be in a type of clothing popular just before the First World War.

Mrs Atkinson assumed they were strangers, obviously attending church after some recent family bereavement. She had no cause to think otherwise, for their figures were completely normal, except for their rather outdated appearance.

At one stage in the service she noticed that the boy was weeping. The woman bent her head over him and put her arm around him, pressing his face hard against her in a comforting hug. Mrs Atkinson was immediately aware of the great sadness of the child, and wondered what possibly could have happened to have caused it.

Prayer time came, and, when she opened her eyes again, the couple had gone. Assuming that they must have left quietly, she thought no more about it, but when the service ended she asked the verger about the sad couple dressed in old fashioned rusty black. But, although he had been sitting in the same pew as Mrs Atkinson, the verger had seen no figures at all other than the regular worshippers, and it was only then that she realised that the emotions she had seen were very much of the past.

A Kindly Ghost

Not very far along one of the main roads leading from the city stands a farm house in which, some years ago, occurred a most interesting case of a ghost which spoke, something which rarely happens. This is the story which was given to me by a lady who, for the sake of privacy, will be referred to as Freda.

In 1943 she was living in this house with her father and mother, and her bedroom was at the front of the house. One night she awoke with the feeling that someone was trying to attract her attention. When she opened her eyes the room was filled with a light brighter than that produced by any normal means of illumination, and standing in front of her was a man, a complete stranger to her.

He had pale gold hair, was handsome and looked extremely clean. Freda noticed that his hands were white and well cared for, certainly not the hands of anyone used to hard manual work. She cannot remember any details about his clothes, other than that his shirt also was particularly clean and white.

He had a kind face, and she felt that he needed help. She sat up and said, "Who are you? What do you want?". Even though the room was so light, at this point she automatically reached up to press the button of the switch that hung over her bed.

Quickly he moved towards her and, although no sound could be heard, his lips framed the words "Oh, no!" and his face showed deep emotion, as though he was disappointed because she was letting him down. His hand reached over her in an attempt to stop her from pressing the switch, and again she noticed the particular whiteness of his skin.

But Freda's movements had anticipated his, and, as her electric light clicked on, the other light faded and she realised she was alone in the room.

Now thoroughly frightened, she screamed. Her father came into the room and, in spite of his anger at the disturbance, had to sleep in her place for the rest of the night whilst she went to her mother's bed. Explanations at breakfast were given but not accepted, both her parents assuring her that she had dreamed the whole incident.

Freda knew that this was not the case. It was all too vivid, although she never saw the figure again. But, on a later occasion she was walking along a path at the front of the house when a voice suddenly called, "Freda! Stop!". Startled, she did so, and as she looked around to see who had called or where the voice had come from, a huge piece of tiling fell from the roof in front of her. No-one was in the house, the garden, or anywhere near, but she feels strongly that she owes her life to whoever or whatever it was. She has also had a sad awareness that perhaps she had been helped by the pale young man who had a short time before been seeking some help from her, help that she had been too frightened to give.

And there the story might have ended. Freda and her family left the farm and for two or three years her strange experience was never mentioned. One night, however, at a family gathering of friends and relations, the subject of mysterious happenings was discussed and, after some general conversation, Freda's father surprised them all by telling them of something strange that had happened to him.

After the disturbance in the night when Freda first saw the pale young man, her father had moved into her bed. As soon as he put out the light he knew that there was a presence with him in the room and, for the first time in his life, he was scared. At breakfast the next morning he told his wife what had happened. It was identical in every way to what had happened to Freda!

He and his wife had decided not to mention this to their daughter so that she would not be frightened, so Freda had never known of her father's confirmation of what she had seen. And then her mother added extra information. Some time previously two Irish workers, a man and a woman, had been employed to help with the sugar beet harvest. They had been given the bed and the room that was normally Freda's, and the woman had complained that there was, as she put it, "a kind of spookiness about it". Freda's mother laughed it off, and so was never given the details, but obviously whatever had happened had caused great alarm, and the Irish workers left very quickly.

Round and About

One of the most frustrating things about collecting ghost stories is the problem of the incomplete story, fragments of information in books or conversation about which no details can be found. Some of these brief references are, however, given here in the hope that readers may know more about them than I have been able to discover, and I shall certainly welcome any help in recording these more fully.

Castlegate has at least two ghosts. One, a lady in grey, thought to be a Quaker, is said to haunt Castlegate House which was the original building of the Mount School. The other resides at No. 6.

Reports have been made of a mysterious figure in a ragged cloak haunting the site of the three-legged mare (the old gallows at Tyburn on Knavesmire).

The old buildings of St Mary's Hospital are said to be frequently visited by a former nursing sister, continuing her earthly work of comforting the seriously ill.

A lady, living in a house not far from Monk Bar, is said, some years ago, to have heard the rattle of ghostly chains on frequent occasions.

In Haxby Road there is, or was, a stile leading into Bootham Stray, where a girl has waited for two hundred years for her lover who failed to turn up.

Strange shadows are said to appear next to the site of the "New Drop", the gallows of York Castle, near the exterior wall facing Castle Mills Bridge.

The Glen, Heworth, was the setting for a ghost which appeared at a Christmas party some years ago. A lady, who wishes to remain anonymous, tells me that she was going up the stairs closely followed by her hostess when they both saw a grey figure in flowing garments come through a door at the top of the stairs, then turn to the right and walk along a landing before disappearing.

A former off-licence shop in Walmgate, demolished in recent years, was reported to have an atmosphere of great evil from time to time.

A Mrs Cooper contacted me, and was able to give me details of other ghost stories of her experience. She told me of the strange happening to a group of children on Acomb Green some years back when Mrs Cooper and about ten other children saw a woman in white. She had a hood over her head, and a long flowing gown. First she walked from the double gates, then disappeared. A friend, who had seen nothing, didn't believe the story, and went with about three others who suddenly saw the same figure standing by the memorial, her head bowed, and her hands clasped as though praying. Other people have also seen the figure in the same position, but there are no details available.

Another experience related by Mrs Cooper is that of a ghostly Labrador seen on the bar walls. Some years ago a gang of thugs pushed the dog off the walls where it fell in front of a lorry and was killed instantly, yet it has still been seen guarding the walls close to the place of its death.

Staff at Middlethorpe Hall (when it was being used as a nightclub) also reported strange uneasiness in certain parts of the building, though so far as can be discovered only one person has actually seen a figure. This was that of a lady whom he often saw watching him from a corner. Her name, traditionally, is Lady Mary, and it is said that she was murdered many years ago by her son who strangled her and then threw her body from the balcony.

An interesting letter came from Canada relating to the experience of Mrs F. Wagner who visited York with her husband in March 1973. It was about noon on a sunny but rather chilly day, and the streets were fairly quiet. The Wagners had been walking round the outside of the walls, and now re-entered the city through Bootham Bar and were going towards the Minster. Just as they had crossed through the archway, Mrs Wagner glanced across the street and saw a nun with a brown faded habit and a white collar heading towards the gate. The letter continues:

"I called my husband's attention to look over, but she seemed to have just vanished into thin air. After returning to Durham, where we were staying with a doctor friend who is a Catholic, I described the nun in great detail and asked which order would be wearing it. He assured me that this particular habit is non-existent. On the way back to Canada we visited Westminster Abbey and there - kneeling beside a casket of an English Queen - was my nun in exactly the habit I described, chiselled in stone. It became clear to me that I must have seen "my ghost" in York."

Footsteps through the Corridors of Time

Just inside Bootham Bar stands an old house which, until the 1920s, was used as a hairdresser's shop. The owners, William and Emma Siddall, lived above the business for many years, and their great-nephew, Mr J.I. Stockton, kindly gave me the following story of their experiences.

The house, like most of the property in the row, is very old. Some of it is built on the site of the medieval church of St Sepulchre, and not very far away is the Board Inn where, in 1816, excavations revealed cellars which had evidently been used as dungeons. A stone cavity was discovered in the walls in which rusty chains and manacles still hung, and traditions tell of underground tunnels leading to the Minster - hence the popular name, "The Hole in the Wall".

At the time the Siddalls lived there, many more pubs existed, and the neighbourhood was considered unsafe for young ladies. Mr Stockton's grandmother often went to baby-sit for the Siddalls, and, because of possible trouble from drunks, she was always carefully locked in. The only door to the premises opened directly onto the pavement, so the girl always accompanied her aunt and uncle to the door and made sure that it was securely locked. It always was, for the Siddalls were extremely careful, and would call out to their niece to make sure that the door was firm on her side.

The Siddalls usually returned about eleven o'clock, but one night about ten o'clock, when the children had long been in bed, their niece heard the bell ring as the shop door opened. Footsteps crossed the shop floor and climbed the first flight of stairs. They paused on the small landing and then continued up the next flight to where the bedrooms were, but, as the footsteps reached the top landing, the sound of them gradually faded away.

Some time later the Siddalls returned. All was in order and the door was firmly locked. They climbed the stairs and opened the living room door. Before their baby-sitter could speak, Mrs Siddall looked at her and said, "Don't say anything, I know what has happened". It turned out that the Siddalls, although often hearing the footsteps themselves, had not wished to alarm their niece by telling her about them. It is interesting that she heard the footsteps on other occasions when she was alone in the house except for the children, yet was never able to find anything to account for them.

It is strange how often mysterious footsteps form part of ghost stories. Not very far away from the building just described is another house which has a tradition of ghostly footsteps. These are interesting in that the sound is exactly like the slap of sandalled feet on a stone floor, even though the room in which the phenomenon occurs is closely fitted with carpets. Even more surprising is the fact that the sound has been localised as being in mid-air, three feet above the present level of the room.

Another interesting anecdote tells of a small girl who asked, "Who walks about in the room when there's nobody there?".

Yet another example concerning footsteps and stairs was told to me by Sir Ivo Thomson, son of Lady Thomson, whose experiences are given elsewhere in this book. Sir Ivo was born, and spent much of his early life at Old Nunthorpe on the Bishopthorpe Road. Originally this had been two houses, but was later made into one dwelling with communicating doors in the basement and on the ground floor. The upper floors of the two houses were, for some reason, not altered and so could be reached only by using the appropriate staircases.

Sir Ivo tells me that shortly before the first World War, he was delighted to find on returning from school that he had been given a small room on the ground floor at the northern end of the house for his own use as a private study. This was a great thrill, and a privilege which he greatly appreciated. Yet, soon after moving in, he discovered that for some inexplicable reason he just could not use it, however much he tried, and eventually he abandoned the room altogether.

Wartime economies caused that part of the house to be shut off, and even when peace came it was only partially reopened. The family at this time often sat in the inner hall, at one end of which was a large archway and through this there was a full view of the stairs. On many occasions as he sat there in the evenings they heard the sound of footsteps coming up from the basement, crossing the hall, climbing the stairs and then walking about in the room above. They referred to the phenomenon as "the old man", but none of them ever saw anything, though it would seem that the dogs, often very perceptive in such matters, either saw or sensed something, for they would growl and raise their hackles. An interesting detail is that the steps were so heavy that Sir Ivo often played the gramophone to deaden the sound.

Although many people were aware of this phenomenon, no mention of it was made outside the family circle, especially to nervous guests. But two girls, neither of whom knew the story, stayed separately in the house and both said that they had seen an old man climbing the stairs.

Eventually the house was sold for development purposes, and remained empty for some time. Going along Lendal one day, Sir Ivo met the auctioneer and asked what had happened to his old home. "Nothing", replied the agent, "but there have been reports that someone has been seen in the house". The keys had been sent for, and the police had made a thorough search of the premises, but found no trace of any intruder.

57

Sir Ivo, on hearing the story, said that the figure must have been seen at the window next to the front door. "Ah, you've obviously heard about the scare then", said the agent, but this was not the case. It was just the fact that the "old man" always stood there. Poor, sad ghost. Not long after his lonely tenancy, the building was demolished, and now many families occupy the site where once the house, the garden and the old man stood.

Bootham Bar, with the Barbican.

Licensed to sell Spirits

If anyone wanted to have a night out in ghostly company, an extensive pub crawl is quite possible in the city. There is a "skeleton-room" at "Ye Olde Starre Inne" in Stonegate about which there is only the tradition that it is haunted, without any further details being recorded. The same can be said about the "Black Swan" in Peaseholme Green. A figure in white has several times been seen on the stairs of the "York Arms", near the west end of the Minster. Perhaps some more information might be supplied by a customer who knows more than I do about these inns and their stories.

The "Five Lions" in Walmgate has been largely rebuilt, but originally there was an extra floor which held a long narrow apartment. This room had an earth floor and a barred gate leading to it - curious features which are said to have existed from the time when cockfights were held there.

In the early years of the present century, an ostler employed in the inn was climbing the back stairs. In the dim light he passed a woman he took to be the owner's wife, and said goodnight to her. But there was no reply, the figure disappeared, and he realised that he had probably seen the ghost of Green Jenny. Who she was, or why she was so called remains uncertain, and no other record of this phantom has been found, although the daughter of a former licensee said she often saw strange shadows on the stairs of the inn.

No figures have been seen in the "Windmill Hotel" in Blossom Street, but in recent years ghostly activity has been recorded. Footsteps have been heard on the stairs, and, as in a former case, the sound has been that of feet on wooden steps, whilst the present staircase is thickly carpeted. Lights have been switched on in cellars and storerooms, even when the building has been thoroughly checked and locked for security.

A cleaner, busy during alterations, moved out of the way to let, as she thought, a workman pass her on the stairs - there was no-one to be seen when she turned round. A former assistant manager, a non-believer in ghosts, was in a state of complete shock after turning a corner one night and finding himself assailed by an icy cold mist - inside the building - and a barman had exactly the same experience.

Glasses and bottles have shattered and been found in the morning in areas which had been closely examined the night before and then securely locked. No real reasons have been discovered for this phenomenon, although one visitor, knowing nothing of earlier stories, was conscious of the presence of an ostler in eighteenth century costume. There is also a story, said to be in a book on York although I have not been able to discover it, that the inn is haunted by the spirit of a little girl, knocked down and killed by a brewer's dray many years ago.

Strange happenings at the "Cock and Bottle" in Skeldergate have been widely reported. Former licensees told of hearing the sound of a heavy door being forced open, yet found nothing to account for it. Unseen presences were said to be watching carefully, and an indistinct figure wearing a wide-brimmed hat has been seen at one of the tables. A sense of evil has pervaded the place, sometimes powerful enough to freeze people to the spot, and sudden falls in temperature have been noted. The presence seems to object very much to the wearing of crosses and crucifixes.

When Peter and Brenda Stanley moved into the pub just before Christmas, 1973, the strange happenings continued. Brenda became aware one evening of a man with dark curly hair. She saw this figure on several occasions, in various parts of the premises, and felt he might be seeking her help. Pictures have fallen from walls, doors opened mysteriously, or have locked themselves, and small objects such as knives have a strange habit of disappearing suddenly, only to reappear in the most unlikely places.

The supposed personality responsible for all this activity is George Villiers, second Duke of Buckingham, whose town house once stood in Skeldergate. It was in a small house in the grounds of his mansion that he conducted scientific experiments, some say to try to turn base metal into gold.

He died in a farmhouse which is still standing in Kirkby Moorside, and in his fever begged repeatedly to be taken to York, but he was too ill to make the journey. And so, "Great Villiers died", and, although a pauper and disgraced, his rank meant that he must be taken for burial in Westminster Abbey where he lies in an unmarked grave. London can claim his bones but, it would seem, he is determined that York shall be his spiritual home, and finds in the congenial company of the "Cock and Bottle" his own particular haven.

Streets Broad and Narrow

Bootham to Clifton

The graceful houses of Bootham must surely provide elegant settings for many figures from the past, even though their once peaceful abode is now choked with the noise and fumes of traffic. Yet there are times, late at night or in the early hours of the morning, when the atmosphere of the past can still be sensed, and fashionably dressed ghosts would come as no surprise if anyone were to meet them.

Not far from the Gillygate end of Bootham stands an old house, now divided into two shops. One part of the building has a magnificent staircase. The house itself has been an old coaching inn, a bank, and even, it is said, a temporary prison, where criminals awaiting more secure accommodation were locked in one of the attic rooms.

Mrs Pickering lived in this house for ten years, and it was she who first told me of its reputation. For many years people heard mysterious footsteps on the stairs, and none of the women folk would ever stay alone in the house. Mrs Pickering told me that after her family had moved elsewhere she met by chance some young men who were lodging on the top floor. They too had been disturbed by the footsteps, although they had not been told of the experience of others. One man, alone in his room, heard the footsteps on the stairs and saw a light shining through his own room. Thinking it was his colleague, he opened the door, but all was in darkness and the landing empty.

Another large house further along the road, now divided into flats, has a cupboard which opens each night at the same time, and people living there have seen the door handle turning when no-one has been outside. Another family I have heard of, living in one of the most attractive houses in the area, has grown so used to the ghost they hear entering their rooms that he has become part of the family, a welcome visitor, whom they would miss if ever he decided to leave!

Two unfounded traditions are passed from generation to generation of pupils in St Peter's School. Late at night, they claim, a grey lady can be seen walking along the road beside the school chapel. The other ghost is also connected with the chapel itself - the ghost of the organ loft. This restless soul shuffles about in red carpet slippers, having haunted this spot ever since the time when, as a pupil at the school, he leaned too far over the edge of the loft and fell to his death.

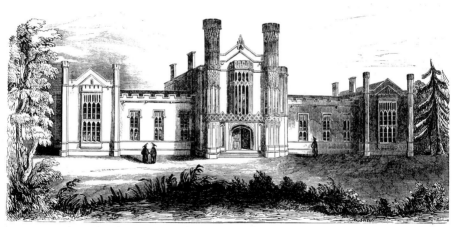

THE YORK PROPRIETARY SCHOOL.

Ethel, Lady Thomson, has an interesting story to tell of the time she saw a ghost in her old home, Clifton Lodge, which stands at the junction of Shipton Road and Rawcliffe Lane. Her experience is yet another example of the surprising number of references to stairs in ghost stories. She was on her way to bed one evening when she saw a figure at the top of the stairs. She thought it was a maid and followed her into one of the main bedrooms. Here the figure went round the side of a wardrobe and disappeared through a locked door into the next room. The same figure was seen in the hall and the dining room, and Lady Thomson and her sisters often heard bumps on the back stairs, and a child crying where no child could possibly be in or near the house.

Before being extended into a large family home, Clifton Lodge was a farm. A servant gave birth to an illegitimate child which she killed, and her spirit has haunted the place ever since.

Stonegate to Coney Street

Also from Lady Thomson's book comes a story concerning Stonegate. Underneath the stairs of one of the overhanging houses a human skull was found some years ago. Whose skull was never discovered, but the ghost who haunted the house was certainly wearing the wide skirted dress of former years. No-one ever saw the lady, so, it might be asked, how did they know it was a lady with a wide skirt? The answer is intriguing. The family owned a cat, an affectionate animal that had a habit of walking in a two foot circle round people as it looked up at them. One day it was noticed that the cat was on the landing, looking at something which was not visible to human eyes - and making a six foot circle, obviously round the wide skirt of the ghost it was welcoming.

Not many people notice the many little alleys which lead off Stonegate. One of these, Church Passage, used to have two or three houses down it, and it was here that Mrs Newton lived as a girl in the first World War. Her father had gone into the army, and she and her mother had only been in the house for about a week when they noticed a strange phenomenon. Every evening, about ten o'clock, they would hear something coming down the entrance hall. Next would come a sound like the swish of a cloak being thrown over one shoulder, and the footsteps would climb the stairs. For two minutes or so there would be silence, then would come a terrible noise as though something (or someone) had been thrown heavily to the floor. Mrs Newton wondered if it could have been the ghost of Guy Fawkes, and says that she would have loved to have seen him. So would we. It would be pleasant to think that York had amongst its ghostly population at least one of its famous citizens.

At one time it was thought that the Mansion House was haunted. A former Mayor and Mayoress heard the sound of heavy footsteps on many occasions as they lay in bed. The Mayoress in particular was convinced that a ghost was around, but investigations disproved so romantic a notion - the footsteps turned out to be those of the night watchman on duty in the department store next door!

A jeweller's shop in Coney Street was the setting for poltergeist activity some years back. Boxes were moved mysteriously, lights were switched on and off, and the staff were disturbed in many different ways, but all is now quiet.

The Mansion-House.

North Street

The last place one might expect a ghost in York would be in one of the newest buildings, but the Viking Hotel can claim an additional visitor - or resident. Staff have reported a vague shape on the stairs, and one man on regular night duty in the hotel was so disturbed that he left his job for a less exciting position. It seems that the Viking was built on the site of a row of houses in which a murder was committed many years ago. The house had always been considered haunted, though it was thought that the ghost might vanish with the demolition of the house, but evidently this was not so. Still, it is pleasant to think that the wraith had such an improvement in its living - or dying - conditions!

All Saints' Church in North Street is a most fascinating building which doesn't always seem to attract the attention of tourists, which is a pity for it is well worth many visits. Although it has lost many of its residents in the parish, services are still held in it; its congregation has always been devout, and devoted.

Mr Tony Walker, who used to own a most attractive and interesting shop selling Yorkshire crafts in the Odeon Buildings, was educated in York and was for a time a member of this congregation. He left to go to university, and eventually became a priest, member of a religious order, and the author of important books on theology. He told me that on Christmas Eve 1953 his mother and a group of friends went to the midnight mass at All Saints' and he, attending another city church, arranged to meet them afterwards. He turned by the corner from Tanner Row where there is a small secluded garden, and saw sitting there a lady whom we will call Harriet. She crossed to the railings and greeted him, using a particular nickname used only by her, and wishing him a Merry Christmas. He replied to her greeting, but seeing his friends coming out of the church, had no time to linger and walked on to rejoin them as they turned into North Street, mentioning to his mother that he had just seen Harriet. Mrs Walker remembers this incident and was able to confirm the details, in particular the fact that it was not until the end of January that she and Tony heard the news that Harriet had died - in November of the previous year!

Goodramgate

Goodramgate is one of York's Danish street names, called after Guthrum, one of the leaders of the period. Its unusual curve has been attributed to the detour that citizens had to make to avoid the piles of rubble left after the burning of the Minster in the days of the Normans. In this street stands a fine Tudor house now used as a café. This is a building which I know well, having stayed there over a period of time, unfortunately without experiencing any of the phenomena which have since been reported. The house, originally built in 1512, was sympathetically restored by the late Cuthbert Morrell, who did so much for the history of the city. During the restoration much fine timbering was revealed, and, in an upstairs room, the name and dates

"Marmaduke Buckle"

1715

1697

17

All Saints, Northstreet.

were found scratched on the plaster work. This inscription was preserved behind a glass frame, and has always fascinated visitors.

Research has shown that Marmaduke, member of a well known York family who owned the house in the seventeenth century, was a cripple who, despairing of his existence, hanged himself from the main beam of the upper room, which runs the whole length of the house.

Strange happenings have included the opening of doors, switching on the lights, and unseen presences on the stairs. As already stated, none of these occurrences were witnessed by the previous tenant of the building or myself, but we were at the same time often aware of an air of sadness in the top room. The rest of the building had a most comforting, pleasant atmosphere, and has for many years been a most popular and busy restaurant. It may well be that Marmaduke still protects his old home, for the charming lady, Jessie Ellis, who for many years lived there, tells me that she was never afraid, even when living alone throughout the war years.

The Beningborough Tragedy

In 1670, Beningborough Hall was a fine Elizabethan mansion, red-bricked and mullioned, its tall, twisted chimneys rising above a parkland bordered by the Ouse and the Nidd. It was tenanted by a family called Earle, but was rarely used by them, for Mr Earle, involved in the religious quarrels of the time, found it wiser to remain in hiding elsewhere, leaving the running of the house to his staff.

The housekeeper, Marian, was a comely rather than pretty woman in early middle age. Like her employer she was a devout Roman Catholic and for this reason was trusted by the family with many of their secrets. It came as no surprise to her when two men arrived with orders to pack all that was most valuable and easy to carry away. This was soon done, but word was awaited as to when the boxes could be moved to France. Marian suggested that for the time being they should be stored in the cottage of the gamekeeper, Martin Giles, to whom she was engaged. He too was a loyal servant and a fellow Roman Catholic. It was an ideal place, so, once the goods were safely in his care, the two men returned to London.

Some time later the steward of the house, Philip Laurie, returned. He was angry at the disappearance of the valuables and accused Marian of having stolen them, but she scorned his suspicion. Knowing of her attachment to Martin Giles, he decided to investigate, and was rewarded by the sight of the boxes in the cottage. He determined to steal the goods so conveniently packed and contacted a local layabout called William Vasey to assist him.

In addition to this plan, Laurie determined to be revenged on Marian, towards whom he felt great bitterness. He knew that she was in the habit of walking along a beech avenue in the evening, saying the rosary as she went. So Vasey watched and waited and as Marian approached, looking down as she told her beads, he sprang from behind a tree and threw her into the river.

When her body was found next day, it was at first thought that she had committed suicide. She was still clutching part of he rosary, but a broken portion wound round the jagged stump of a fallen tree, and an imprint of a man's boot in the mud soon showed that her death was neither accidental nor self-inflicted. More footprints behind a bush showed that someone had been hiding there, awaiting Marian. Probably because his manner over the past few days had been secretive, suspicion surprisingly fell on Marian's lover.

Playing on this suspicion, Laurie and Vasey decided on their next assault - the theft of the goods, and the murder of Martin. Vasey, an experienced burglar, broke into the cottage, leaving Laurie to keep watch outside. But Martin, grieving for Marian, was still awake. Although he was stunned for a time by a blow on the head, he managed to throw a sheep net over his attacker and fire a musket through the window to warn the other servants at the hall.

They came running, and with them came Philip Laurie, pretending to have been alarmed by the sound of the gun. A tremendous struggle followed, during the course of which Laurie managed to swear William Vasey to secrecy before the latter was finally captured and committed to York Castle on charges of burglary and attempted murder.

When the news of this turmoil at Beningborough reached London, Mrs Earle travelled north. She soon realised that Philip Laurie's behaviour was suspicious. Why, for example, was he fully dressed after midnight? Suspicious she might be, but could prove nothing. Nevertheless she dismissed him from her service and also told him that William Vasey was determined to make a full confession in York.

Laurie, in desperation, flung himself at her feet, and begged her to let him go with her to France, where she was expecting to join her husband. She refused, adding that she could no longer trust him, whereupon he drew a pistol from his pocket, and aimed it at her head. Mrs Earle, used to living in danger, was a courageous woman, and struck the pistol upwards just as it fired, the bullets shattering a chandelier in the centre of the ceiling. Terrified and bewildered, Laurie, whose mind was obviously unbalanced, rushed from the room, seized another pistol in his own apartment and blew out his brains.

William Vasey was brought to trial, an event which caused tremendous local interest. He was condemned, and his execution attracted great crowds. The nearness of the tragedy, and Marian's popularity, had caused every detail of the case to be discussed. But the excitement of the crowd was to be heightened for, on August 18th, 1670, William Vasey, as he stood at the Tyburn on Knavesmire, made full confession and his hanging closed the case.

Or did it? It would seem not, for, soon after the tragedy, people began to see a pale, neat figure, walking along the banks of the Ouse. Her head was bent, and in her hands were the beads. A tall, gentle lady, who kept her head down as she walked, before eventually disappearing in the churchyard of Newton-on-Ouse, where the faithful Marian lay buried, close to the park of Beningborough Hall which she had served so well.

Treasurer's House

B orley Rectory is said to have been "The Most Haunted House in England". If such a title were awarded in York, the prize must surely go to Treasurer's House which has provided, by numbers at any rate, the most exciting activity of the supernatural related so far.

The first case, the ghost of George Aislaby, is another haunting connected with duelling. The Aislaby family, who also owned Fountains Hall, had bought Treasurer's House from Lord Fairfax. By January 1674 the Aislabys were well established, and on January 10th, with Mary Mallorie, co-heiress of Studley, they attended a ball at the Duke of Buckingham's house in Skeldergate.

Miss Mallorie, enjoying herself, stayed late with the man to whom she was betrothed, Jonathan Jennings, and missed the servant who had been sent to escort her home. Jonathan therefore took her in his own carriage.

Unfortunately, when they reached Treasurer's House, repeated knockings failed to wake anyone, so that Mary had to spend the night with a relative of her fiancé, and next day "high words" passed between him and her brother-in-law, George Aislaby. High words led to a quarrel, a quarrel to a blow, and a blow to a challenge. As the Minster bell struck for the morning service, a duel was fought in nearby Penley Crofts. George Aislaby, mortally wounded, was carried home to die. Jonathan Jennings was shocked to hear of the death of his adversary and, borrowing a coach from the Duke of Buckingham, hurried to London to obtain pardon from Charles II. He later returned to York, though Miss Mallorie, the cause of the original quarrel, never married him, or anyone else.

George Aislaby was buried in the Minster, not far from the choir screen, but, it is said, his ghost continues to haunt Treasurer's House. An interesting link with this case was given to me some time ago. A man who regularly used Chapter House Street reported that, whenever he passed the door of Treasurer's House, he felt an acute sense that he must protect himself from some violent attack. Should he be walking with anyone else this feeling increased considerably, even though he knew nothing of the Aislaby story at that time.

In 1897 fine seventeenth century panelling was discovered under layers of wallpaper in the Tapestry Room on the first floor. A careful restoration was made, but, although it is a large and important room, people never cared to use it afterwards. It had a gloomy atmosphere, and always felt much colder than the rest of the building. Exactly when this atmosphere began is no longer known, but it is said to have been after a wife, driven to despair by the cruelty of her husband, murdered him when he threatened to introduce his mistress into the house to live with them. But, as no-one has ever seen the ghostly visitant, it is uncertain whether it is the erring husband or the unhappy wife who returns to the scene of the tragedy.

The most remarkable story of the hauntings in York in recent years must surely be the events which were recorded by Harry Martindale in the early nineteen fifties. At that time alterations to the premises were going on, together with archaeological surveys. Harry, an apprentice aged about 17, had been working in one of the cellars, installing piping for central heating. He was standing on a short ladder when he first heard the sound of a trumpet. He paid little attention to this, other than feeling slight surprise that the sound of a brass band should have reached him where he was working, but the sound drew nearer and nearer, and suddenly the figure of a horse came through the wall. It was large and lumbering - its fetlocks heavy and shaggy. Harry fell from his ladder to the earth floor in a state of confusion and shock. More was to come. On the back of the horse was a man dressed in Roman costume, and behind him came a group of soldiers, not marching in formation, but shuffling in a dispirited way, with their heads down. They took no notice of Harry as he lay on the floor, but the details of their appearance were to remain with him.

Treasurer's House

69

He was surprised by their small stature, and shabby appearance. He described with great detail the rough, home-made clothes they were wearing. The sandals, cross gartered to the knees, were very badly made, and their kilted skirts, green in colour, gave the impression that they had been roughly dyed. They carried round shields (an unusual feature in the Roman army), long spears and short swords. He cannot remember any banner or standard, but the trumpet was very clear, a long straight instrument, much used and battered. The finest part of their equipment appeared to be the helmets, with fine plumes of undyed feathers.

The portion of the cellar they were in is low and narrow, and is 18 inches above the level of the old Roman road which the archaeologists had recently uncovered, together with a fallen column from the headquarters building. At one stage, when the horse was first coming through the wall, the group appeared to be without legs, but were later seen to be walking on the original level of the Roman road itself. Still with this air of utter dejection, the group crossed the cellar, and silently disappeared through the opposite wall.

Shocked and trembling, he rushed up the cellar steps to the ground floor. Here he stumbled across the curator who, noticing his agitation, said, "You've seen the Romans, haven't you?". This remark was of great comfort, as Harry then realised that he had neither been seeing things nor was going out of his mind. At the suggestion of the curator he wrote down what he had seen, and was later astonished to find that two other people had also left accounts, giving identical details.

For over twenty years he kept quiet about his strange experience. A few close friends had been told and some details had been given, but it was not until 1974 that he could be persuaded to make public what had happened to him. Harry became P.C. Martindale, an honest and discriminating citizen who would scorn to add anything to his story that didn't actually happen. He has been questioned by experts in Roman history, who have been impressed by the details he has given. Throughout he assured them that his previous ideas of Roman soldiers were derived only from Hollywood epics and did not fit in with what he actually saw in the cellars. And through it all comes his puzzled cry, "Why me? I wasn't interested in either ghosts or Romans!".

Nor did he know of another story from Treasurer's House. When it was still being used as a private house, Mr Frank Green, who later gave it to the National Trust, was a generous host. On one occasion he held a fancy dress party in the house. During a lull in the merriment, an opportunity was given for the guests to explore the house. One young lady, Eve Fairfax, being more venturesome than the rest, found her way into the cellars. Perhaps a game of hide and seek was in process - for she certainly seems to have wandered far from the others. Coming across a passage, she was about to go along it when she saw a guest dressed as a Roman soldier. Along she went, but the figure barred further progress by placing his spear across the archway. He said nothing, but his action made it quite clear that she was not to go on. Puzzled, and somewhat annoyed by his peremptory manner, she returned upstairs and asked her host which of his guests had come dressed as a Roman. Equally puzzled, he told her that no-one was wearing anything remotely resembling such a disguise. Was this another example of the history of York being recorded on her many beautiful buildings?

To have had an experience such as Harry Martindale's sighting of the Roman soldiers was remarkable - but to find an independent witness of the same happenings was more than I could ever have hoped for, and yet it was to be.

It was some years since I had met the next witness, but I was delighted to see her at one of the talks that I was giving at a York hotel. We chatted over old times, but had to finish our reminiscences when the lunch began. As usual I talked about the Roman soldiers last, and as usual people were intrigued by this strange happening. As the guests were leaving I met my friend Joan again. She was kind enough to say how much she had enjoyed the talk and then, almost casually, said, "Of course, you know I've seen the Romans as well".

It was an electrifying moment, but unfortunately I had to leave, and it was some time before I was able to make a recording. Joan, as she wishes to be called, is a charming person and an effective witness, who makes no claims to be psychic in any way. Like Harry she had no particular interest in Romans, or belief in ghosts, and yet, in round about 1957, she too was to be made vividly aware of both.

At that time she and her husband were living in Treasurer's House in an official capacity, with their ward, Caroline, then a young girl. Although they enjoyed being there and found it a beautiful house, it had not, at that stage, been fully restored and modernised. Joan remembers in particular how cold it was, with only partial central heating - and a lack of hot water above stairs. The old-fashioned heating apparatus had to be stoked frequently and a boiler man usually saw to this, but not at the week-ends.

One very cold and miserable Sunday - in February as she remembers it, sometime in the late afternoon or early evening period - Joan went into the cellar to check the boiler. She was, as usual, accompanied by her faithful bull terriers who went everywhere with her. Suddenly the dogs stopped and refused to go into the cellars, bristling and growling angrily. Joan was astonished at this unusual behaviour - even more so when the animals turned tail and fled howling, and stood whining dismally at the top of the stairs leading from the courtyard into the old kitchen.

She opened the door leading to the cellars, and entered the low, rather dark tunnel off which was the boiler room. As she went she heard the sound of horses' hooves but assumed the sound came from Chapter House Street above her head. Suddenly she realised that she was no longer alone. Something or someone was in the tunnel behind her. She was petrified and, wondering what on earth was happening, huddled against the wall.

It was then that she saw for the first time a group of Roman soldiers travelling along the tunnel in the direction of the Minster. Like Harry she could not see the lower parts of the legs of the men and horses, but unlike Harry she never did see the figures completely. It would seem that the group was travelling on the level of the Roman road, eighteen inches below the present floor in the cellar - but the part she was in had not been excavated, unlike the small cellar where Harry had been.

She was so petrified that she doesn't remember clear details of what she encountered, but even so it is obvious that it was a similar but not identical experience to that of Harry's. The number of figures she saw was not definite, but there were four or five horses on the far side of the group that passed her. The men, most of whom were leading the horses, were tired, dishevelled and dirty. The figures seemed perfectly solid and real, and she noticed particularly the details of the reins and harness. Had she not been so frightened she feels she could have put out her hand and touched the figures, yet she was seeing them in some strange way through the brickwork of the tunnel which had unaccountably disappeared.

In a state of shocked amazement, she stayed until the figures rounded the end of the tunnel. Reality returned, and she became aware of the crying of her dogs at the top of the stairs. They knew only too well what was happening below. She stayed for some time in the tunnel, trying to puzzle out what had happened and what she had seen. She had no-one to turn to - her husband was unwell, and she certainly didn't want to worry the child Caroline, so she never mentioned the experience to anyone.

Subsequently she saw the strange procession again - in fact on two or three occasions. Although the basic details and timing were the same, the sightings were not identical. The horses were in the background on the first occasion, on the second they were nearly all being led, on the third occasion the men were all on horseback, but not in a riding position. Then they seemed so exhausted that they were leaning forward as though asleep on the horses' necks. The horses themselves were splashed with mud, and the whole dispirited group appeared as though it was returning from a very long and difficult journey.

Joan became so disturbed by these experiences that eventually she would never go into the cellars again. She still believed her story to be unique, and is adamant that she never heard any stories about strange happenings anywhere in

Treasurer's House. She knew of its royal connections, and did admit to a general feeling of a strange atmosphere in Princess Victoria's room - but that was all.

The years went by. Joan left Treasurer's House, and Caroline married and is now living in Australia. On one occasion they were talking of earlier days in Treasurer's House when Caroline suddenly said, "Oh, didn't that trumpet sound loudly!" For the first time, Joan realised that she had not been alone in her experience. Although she had never seen anything, Caroline as a child had often heard the muffled sound of the trumpet and the hooves of the horses. The odd thing is that she heard the sound when she was in her bedroom - right at the top of the house.

The story became part of Joan's past. She never mentioned it to anyone else, she never heard any talk, read any account or saw any television account until she heard my lunch-time talk several years after she had left Treasurer's House. It wasn't until she heard me mention the experience of Harry Martindale that she realised that she hadn't been alone - in any sense of the word!

St William's College

The following story is, I think, worth recording. It is taken from a book called "Wortlebank Diary" by the Victorian writer, Holme Lee, whose real name was Harriet Parr. Although she gives different names to the city, the Minster and the ancient college itself, internal evidence shows that she was describing York, and using one of the traditional stories of the haunting of St William's College.

This story had been thought to be mere fiction but the sound of footsteps in empty rooms, latches raised by unseen hands and the sound of heavy objects being dragged across the floor have all been reported in recent years.

Many years ago there lived in St William's College an engraver called Nicholas Drew, a quiet, inoffensive old man who minded his own business, though he was of a charitable nature. He occupied the whole of one of the upper floors which he reached, not by the common staircase, but by a flight of steps he had made under the centre window. Other residents of the college were puzzled why he used the six rooms he rented. He seemed to live in sordid poverty, but gossip said that he had great wealth hidden in the locked rooms. Other people talked grimly of black magic.

Nicholas had a stern, somewhat unkindly face, not unlike one of the carved heads on the corbel of the gateway. Sharp eyes peered anxiously from beneath his brow. Lank hair curled down onto his collar from his high forehead, and his beard was dishevelled. His worn, patched clothing was always hidden beneath a dusty tartan cloak, and his small, nervous figure, with its rapid gait, was a source of scorn and amusement to all who saw him.

He generally chose wet days or the hours of twilight to go out and about on his business. Under his cloak he carried a portfolio of prints and engravings. His head was covered with a wide brimmed felt hat, big enough to serve as an umbrella. Mocking urchins threw stones at him, always keeping a safe distance. Yet he had a warm heart and longed for friendship and companions. His sensitive nature shrank from the universal hatred and mockery which he seemed to inspire, and he could never understand why everyone shunned his company.

One snowy New Year's Eve Nicholas crept out to visit a printseller in the city with an etching of the Chapter House which he had just finished. The wind was high, and blinding snowflakes drove full into his face. He turned his back on the Minster and trudged into Petergate. The shop was closed when he got there, so he knocked and knocked. A surly youth appeared eventually and said that his master had guests and would not be disturbed.

"I'll call tomorrow then", said Nicholas.

"Don't bother. Master says he's changed 'is mind. Yer pictures are too dear." The door slammed in his face.

Sadly Nicholas turned to go home. Passing along Petergate he met a crouching, ragged figure, begging for money in a hoarse and feeble voice. "Master, for the love of heaven, for the love of the mother that bore you, help me." Nicholas had little enough for himself, so pushed her aside, and went on his way. Yet, as he walked, the reference to his mother moved him and he turned back in search of the old woman. Eventually he found her standing on the bridge, contemplating suicide. "It's an easy death", she said.

"It is nothing of the sort", it is dreadful", cried Nicholas. "It is damnation to listen to such temptation."

"Why not?", asked the old woman. "Why not die at once instead of dying by inches? Who are you to condemn me to live, yet give me no support?"

"You must wait your hour", said Nicholas. "You are not to lift the latch of life yourself and steal away from your sorrows like a thief in the night."

"I am no thief, yet 'tis not easy to pine day after day and to shrink, ragged and ashamed in the streets by night. Children spit at me, and little things that can scarcely walk alone raise shrill cries against me. Don't ever think that you have all the rough bits of life to yourself."

Nicholas had led her from the bridge, and they were now standing at the corner of the market place. "Don't, I pray you, go near the bridge again", he said, pressing a shilling into her hand. It was the last he had.

74

"God bless you, master", she whispered.

The snow thickened, and all the bells of the city seemed alive, clanging and clattering in every direction as Nicholas trudged home. The warmth of her blessing stayed with him as he went, but when he came in sight of the grocer's shop at the corner he had to forget the gnawing emptiness under his tartan cloak. He had nothing now.

Wind, snow and bells together seemed to fill the air and to come tearing down College Street as he went, clutching his cloak around him as he crept under the overhanging timbers of the courtyard. Here he stood in the porch, resting the portfolio in a niche in the wall while he shook the snow from his cloak. Suddenly a sound close at his heels made him jump as if he had been bitten. Could one of his juvenile persecutors have lain in wait for him at such an hour and in such weather?

Alarmed at the thought, he darted across the courtyard to the haven of his own rooms. Here he turned to the refuge of the lonely and began to talk to himself.

"Too bad! I never hurt anyone that I know of. Poor old Nick! You're a sad, miserable, despised old pauper. No - not sad. not miserable, it's not true - it's wrong to mention it." Breaking up a lump of coal he poked the fire into a cheerful blaze so that the room was filled with a dancing radiance. He warmed his wrinkled hands in the glow, and, as the snow on his beard began to melt, so his spirits rose.

"What right have I to complain?" he mused. "Many would be glad of a shelter like this. I wonder what that poor old soul would give to warm herself by such a fire as this. Come now, let's to work."

Suddenly he remembered that he had left his portfolio in the niche. "Now what do I do?" he thought. "Has that little urchin gone to bed yet, I wonder?" Cautiously he descended into the courtyard, grasped his case, and was just about to return when he was startled by the sudden sobbing of a child.

"Why don't you go home to your mammy, little one", he asked gently, stooping over a dark bundle crouching against the wall. There was no answer, other than a hysterical cry from the figure as it shrank away from him.

"You must not stop here all night. You may get frozen to death. Tell me where you live, and I'll carry you there", he said, but, with renewed shrieks and sobs, the child refused to be moved.

"Now what shall I do?" wondered Nick, and rapidly thinking over his neighbours decided to ask help from a woman who had always been a little less uncivil to him than the rest of the inhabitants of the tenements. Luckily he found Mrs Parker still up, and quickly told his tale. Wrapping her shawl around her she crossed the yard with him to see for herself.

"Why", she said, "it's the foreign woodcarver's bairn". Quickly gathering it up, she carried the child to Nicholas's room.

"Where's thi faither, little one?" she asked.

"He's dead", cried the child, weeping bitterly. Mrs Parker gathered the child to her, in warmth and comfort and, once the grief had subsided and the waif had been given bread and milk, it sank into an exhausted sleep on the settee near the fire.

"I wonder if that is true", said Nicholas. "I saw him only today working at the Minster, and yet now the window of his room is dark". He hurried downstairs and knocked loudly at the door in the angle of the courtyard where the woodcarver, Louis Duclos, had rented a tiny room. There was no reply, and further enquiries from neighbours soon proved the truth of the tragedy. Whilst working on some scaffolding in a house, Duclos had fallen to his death.

Immediately Nicholas resolved that he would keep this child, and bring it up as his own. Now she had no-one, and neither had he. This could be the companionship for which he had yearned. How he would manage he did not know, he had nothing in the larder but part of a brown loaf and a pitcher of water, but his determination was strong. As he made his silent vow, the clock struck midnight, the bells stopped, and a new year began.

The years passed and the child, who was called Adie, grew into a strong, vivacious young woman, subject to wild fits of laughter and rarer moments of

76

gloom. She showed no application for work, nor any special talent, yet somehow she transformed the atmosphere of the building. Flowers were planted in the courtyard and in window boxes, and linnets sang in cages. Nicholas's circumstances also improved over the years. He had let some of his rooms, his etchings had sold well and he had also found work as a drawing master at some of the many schools in York. Life was happy, the bond between Nicholas and Adie was strong, and his life and his work prospered..

When Adie was seventeen, however, this happiness ended when she and her guardian quarrelled over the attentions being paid to her by Laurence Royston, a tall slender man with auburn hair, cold flickering eyes, and a mouth which seemed to Nicholas to have a sinister appearance. On the rare occasions he laughed, it was an insincere and unlovely sound, and Nicholas often felt his heart grow cold as though some tragedy lay ahead. He began to spend more and more time alone in a tiny room which had been partitioned off in one corner of the large hall in which he lived. This closet was lit by a very small window, darkened by a veil of smoke and dust like the thickest curtain, giving the room an air of gloomy mystery. The room had in it only a rough table and chair, and a cabinet of great antiquity and curious workmanship which was always kept locked. Nicholas rarely entered this room, but when he did often stayed several hours, and came out with an air of sadness and depression. Adie longed to know what was there, and declared that it was haunted, but never was she allowed to go into it. Many people living in the old college had heard the sound of footsteps and had instinctively shunned this part of the building when night fell. For a long time Adie could discover nothing about the tradition of haunting until eventually Mrs Parker told her the following story.

Many years ago, when the college was used by the clergy, two brothers who lived in the upper rooms murdered a priest. Eventually, the elder brother, to save himself, denounced his younger brother and told the authorities that he was hiding in the oak closet where he had been, in an agony of remorse, since the crime was committed. Having given this information, he returned to the college and, unable to face his doomed brother, paced the corridor to and fro, waiting for the authorities to arrive and arrest the murderer. The younger brother was tried, condemned and hanged, the elder one escaping for having turned king's evidence. But he did not survive long; his guilty soul could find no rest, and his spirit was doomed to walk as long as St William's College stands. The fine old cabinet, inlaid with ivory, belonged to these brothers, and was said to have contained proof of their guilt. Certainly the footsteps seemed to start from the spot where the cabinet stood.

On hearing this story, Adie showed even more interest in the tiny closet and the old cabinet, and eventually Nicholas showed her the room, though he did

77

not offer to unlock the cabinet of inlaid ivory, and her further questions as to its contents were not answered.

Some time later Adie went for a walk by the riverside. It was a calm, beautiful evening. A few red bars crossed the western sky, supported by a low mass of purple cloud. The long grass by the river had just been mown, and the fresh hay gave out a healthy scent. Many people walked there in the evening, and it was here that Adie met with Laurence Royston, exercising his dog. She had not seen him for some time, and as she walked with him she told him the story of the haunted chamber, and how she had heard the footsteps, although she had seen nothing. Royston laughed at her tale. "What kind of steps?" , he asked.

"Slow and solemn, as of a person walking while meditating deeply. The steps are regular and firm, never pausing", she explained.

"Why should a ghost have such solidity of step when it is but an airy nothing?" he asked, but Adie could not explain this, and he quickly lost interest in the tale of the supernatural. He was, however, keenly interested in what Adie had to say about the cabinet with the inlaid ivory. He had often heard rumours that Nicholas had a large amount of money hidden away in his rooms, and Royston now surmised that this could well be in the cabinet in the locked room.

The months passed and winter came once more. In November, Adie heard the mysterious footsteps crossing the floorboards whilst she was in the courtyard, and felt the old atmosphere of happiness was disappearing. Nicholas now openly stated how he distrusted this young man with whom Adie spent so much of her time, and, after a violent quarrel, refused to allow his adopted daughter to see Laurence Royston again. In a fit of jealous rage, Royston, knowing that Adie was visiting friends in another part of the city, forced his way into the upper rooms of the College, and after a bitter quarrel and a short struggle, shot Nicholas, killing him instantly. To give the impression that thieves had broken in and were responsible for the murder, Royston broke open the door of the panelled room and forced open the ivory cabinet, eager to find the fortune inside. Drawer after drawer he wrenched open, but never a coin was to be found. All that the cabinet contained was linen, the clothes of Nicholas's wife and child who, according to an inscription in an old bible, had died of fever many years before.

Then, as the murder turned from the cabinet and re-entered the main room, he heard a sudden noise. Someone was coming, and yet, when he looked, the hall was empty except for the huddled figure of the old man lying in a pool of blood. But the sound was there - clear, steady and unmistakable.

For the first and last time, Laurence Royston had heard the ghostly footsteps of St William's College.

Fresh Haunts and Phantoms New

Since the first edition of this book was published, several interesting stories have come in concerning the area round York rather than the city itself, and these are now included here so that they too will be recorded rather than disappear like so many of the ghosts they describe.

For many of these stories I am deeply indebted to information supplied by Miss Ursula Lascelles of Slingsby, whose encyclopaedic knowledge and meticulous recording of the events of the area she loved have formed a valuable source of the greatest importance to any researchers.

Ghostly Gilling

Gilling Castle had, in years gone by, a ghost which was said to be of a frightful appearance. It was the apparition of a young girl of the Fairfax family who had been scalded to death, either accidentally or, as some say, on purpose by the family nurse.

The old rectory was bought in 1968 by a Dr C.I.R. Pickles who had many alterations made. One of the electricians working there told Miss Lascelles of many strange poltergeist activities whilst the house was being modernised. A cigarette lighter lying on the floor unaccountably disappeared and, although the doctor spent all afternoon looking, it was never found. Whilst the electrician was working in the kitchen, although it was a still, calm day, the back door suddenly flew open, and a large piece of plywood was blown round the kitchen. After an electrician came down from the attics shaking with fright, a carpenter refused to work alone in the house.

Coxwold

In 1925, a new Irish doctor took up residence in Coxwold. He also had friends in Thirsk, and often went over to see them, travelling on his motor cycle. The road he then took was quiet and lonely, with several fords having little footbridges over them. At one of these fords, when returning to Coxwold late at night, he twice saw quite clearly a quaint little old couple. They stood on the plank bridge, clearly visible in the moonlight, and both wearing old fashioned clothes, brass buttons on the man's coat, a bonnet for the little old lady and so forth. And yet, when the doctor approached, there was never anything there.

Waterholmes Farm

This building, which was demolished in 1962, stood near Ness Hall. Many years ago now, Mrs Rose Dixon (née Kendall) and her son Ralph were sitting in the house alone one Sunday night. It was quite dark outside, and they were talking about religious experiences, and discussing the subject of a personal devil. Ralph declared no belief in the existence of such a being, and in a loud voice mockingly cried, "If the Devil is here, let him show himself then!".

Immediately they both heard the sound of a heavy scratching at the door. Ralph rushed to open it, but could see nothing, though he searched carefully round the outside of the house. There was nothing there, not even a sheep dog which lived nearby, so he went back indoors, somewhat puzzled by this strange experience. Next morning, on going out of the house, he suddenly noticed a mark high up on the door, the sort of gash that might have been made if two strong claws had struck the door, deeply scratching the wood. The mark was too high for it to have been made by any animal, nor did the form of the mark suggest that it was someone playing a trick. Had a mischievous neighbour overheard the conversation he might, perhaps, have rapped loudly on the door with a stick, but it is unlikely that he would have been carrying any instrument which could so exactly have given the impression of a clawing movement. No ordinary explanation was ever made for this incident, though it is perhaps not surprising that Ralph was never heard to invoke the Devil again.

Cotton Ball Mally

This strangely named ghost used to frequent the house and family at Ness Hall some years ago, and seemed to have some connection with the Kendalls, for she only came to members of that family when there was some change in their circumstances. Ada Kendall, just before her brother's marriage, told the family that a bat had brushed across her face during the night and wakened her, but, knowing the tradition, other members realised that it must be Mally herself.

Up in the attics of Ness Hall there were stains of blood on some of the floor boards, the trail leading from one attic to another. Tradition says that Cotton Ball Mally was murdered up there for some reason now forgotten. She was a pedlar woman who travelled about selling cotton balls. An older house once stood on the site of Ness Hall, and these attics belonged to that period. A prominent Roman Catholic family, the Craithornes, owned Ness from 1333 until in 1788 they sold it to Thomas Kendall. This would suggest that the ghost must be of that period. A later member of the family had some of the bloodstained boards removed, since when

Mally has been much less evident, though some stains remained, and Mally continued to make herself known if any change was about to happen to the family.

Nunnington

Miss Pickett of Slingsby saw the ghost of a lady in Nunnington Avenue. She was then living with her uncle in Nunnington, and one evening, after church, she decided to visit the Misses Foxton who lived in Ness. She was approaching the cross-roads in the avenue just as it was getting dark, when she saw a woman walking directly towards her. As this person drew near, Miss Pickett thought, "How silly, we shall run into each other". She put out her hands - and walked straight through the oncoming figure! On telling her uncle when she returned home he told her that she must have seen the ghost of Catherine Stamper, a member of a very old Nunnington family who, for some unknown reason, had often been seen haunting that area, walking to and fro.

The story of the disappearance of a little boy at Nunnington Hall has been printed before, but from a lady who lived there as a child came a more recent report that when she was very small a lady often came and lifted her out of bed. This would seem to be the ghost of a former resident of the Hall, searching for her own lost child.

Many years before, the owner of Nunnington was left a widower with an only son. He married a second time, a lady as proud and as cold as she was beautiful. In time she too had a son on whom she lavished all her care and attention, completely neglecting the child of her husband's first marriage. Indeed she seemed to have developed a jealous hatred of this boy and, after the death of her husband, treated the lad with great cruelty.

Her step-son was, for the most part, shut up in an upper room, the walls of which were covered with painted leather, and here he would be visited by his little half brother who grew very fond of him, to the extreme annoyance of his step-mother. One day the room with the painted leather was empty and the boy had gone. No-one could ever discover what had happened to him, though there is in the nearby river a deep area in which it was assumed the child had either fallen or been drowned by his step-mother. Certainly there were no signs of grief or concern from her though her own child was heart broken, and would never believe that his playmate had gone. Hour after hour he would wait gazing out of the window hoping for his friend's return until one evening he leaned out too far, and fell to his death.

After that the proud lady was never happy, and her reason would appear to have gone. She would sit for hours talking to herself in a low voice, then suddenly hurry up the oak stairs to the room of painted leather, and stand gazing out of the window from which her child had fallen. At last she died, but succeeding tenants have often heard the strange sounds - the rustle of a silk dress as a figure hurries up the stairs, footsteps crossing the room towards the window out of which she had so often gazed, and then the slow, sad steps as she once more returned to the floors below. The rustle of her dress has been heard recently by the National Trust custodians.

Claxton Hall

When this was lived in by the Rev. Charles Coates and his family, both they and their servants once heard dreadful screams, but were never able to account for them. There was also in this large and lonely house an atmosphere of intense gloom and despair. The story of the screams was never fully explained, but legend says that the atmosphere probably lingered from the days when Claxton Hall, being in the country, was used as a private asylum. One unfortunate girl was sent here by her brother, who was greedy for her inheritance, and eventually, appalled by the cruelty of the treatment, she threw herself over the balcony into the hall and was killed.

Wigginthorpe Hall

On one occasion when Mr Henry Fitzwilliam and his family were living here, his daughters were out for an evening drive. Lady Mary, the butler and a footman all heard the carriage sweep up the gravel drive and stop outside the front door, but when it was opened there was nothing there, and it was a full half hour before the family did return.

A similar strange occurrence concerned Miss Lascelles' brother, Lionel. Some years back he had saved an old cottage in Sheriff Hutton from demolition, and had it re-thatched. It was then let to a Mr Crowe, a rabbit catcher, on whom Lionel often used to call. On one occasion, Mrs Lascelles and her children had been in York and Lionel had said that he intended to call on Mr Crowe on his way back. This he did, only to be met by a puzzled Mr Crowe who had heard Lionel's special knock - half an hour before, but no-one had been there - and when the latter did knock the Crowes hardly dared to open the door. He took some convincing that it must have been at that very moment that Lionel was in York, having just made up his mind to make the visit.

Haxby

During the war, a Highland postman called John McJannett lived in the village. He certainly was possessed of "the gift" as it was called in his native Scotland, and had several tales of strange happenings. None, perhaps more strange than an event which happened one very wet night when he was driving through Haxby in the direction of York. Suddenly in the dimmed headlights of the van (dimmed because of black-out restrictions) he saw the figure of a very old clergyman standing by the roadside. John stopped and offered the man a lift. "You're a very old man to be out on a wet night like this", remarked the postman. "Yes, I was eighty", said the figure as he was getting out at the vicarage gates. It was not until later that John realised the use of the past tense, and not until later still that he discovered that his passenger had died six months previously.

Sheriff Hutton

When Rev. Lascelles was vicar of Sheriff Hutton, a relative, later Lord Manton, a tall, athletic man, often stayed at the vicarage, and once vaulted over some high iron railings round the house. Many years later his son Mark Watson who was staying at Slingsby asked if he might see the house and the railings, so along they all went. They rang the bell several times, but there was no answer. The house was absolutely quiet, except for the sound of a child inside the house crying - a dreary, desolate cry which seemed to be from a child of about eighteen months old. The party felt so sorry for this child's unhappiness, and wondered that so young a child had been left alone in the house.

On seeing Rev. Nelson and telling him of this experience, they were very surprised when he said that he and his family had been in Scarborough all that day, so that there could have been no child in the house, nor indeed was there any member of his family who was that young. It must, he declared, have been a child from a neighbouring farm, but Miss Lascelles knew only too well that this could not be. The crying had definitely come from a room in the centre of the house.

Sheriff Hutton Castle

One day in early October, a local inhabitant, Mr Jagger of the castle farm, saw in the neighbourhood of the castle a group of ladies and gentlemen dressed in the style of former years, apparitions which had also been reported by other people including a well known Harrogate jeweller. The figures were very real, and the detail of their clothes quite clearly seen. In particular the long, hanging sleeves of the ladies were evident, with a curious plaited ornament rather like a cable-stitch as the only decoration. Such ornamentation was rather unusual, but when a costume expert from London was consulted some years later, he discovered that such a style had indeed been worn for a very short period, at the time, in fact, when the castle was inhabited by the retinue of the Earl of Warwick.

Miss Lascelles has a most beautiful ring from this period that was found in the moat, and it is an interesting fact that recently, someone handling this ring, and not, at the time, knowing the previous story, had much the same impression. Groups of people were walking up and down outside the castle, following some special celebration. It was springtime, and they walked on a level grassy area which could well have been used for a tournament. One of the ladies, who seemed to have been playing a special part in the ceremonies, perhaps as queen of the tournament or even as May Queen, was wearing hanging sleeves. It was a scene of great happiness, and there was much laughter. No further clues as to the period were given, although the names Eleanor and Robert de Faulkner were strongly impressed on his mental image.

Another friend told Miss Lascelles that a Mrs Egerton had one day been in the church when she heard people talking French behind one of the pillars. Thinking that a group of tourists had arrived, she moved round behind the pillar - to find, to her complete astonishment, that the whole church was completely empty. Was it just coincidence that five hundred years ago French was the fashionable language of the lords and ladies who were living at the castle?

Newburgh Priory

Newburgh, one of the loveliest houses of the district, seems, like so many of the stately homes of England, to have its share of ghosts both inside and out.

A phantom lady walks by the side of the ornamental lake, just where the water runs under the road towards the Coxwold end. Legend says that a duel was once fought there because of this lady and that the death of one, or both, of the rivals is the reason for her continuing presence. She has been seen on several occasions, and when Dr McCracken and his groom saw her on one occasion, the shock was so severe that the doctor had to sit up all night with the groom, who was seriously ill for some time after that.

Sir George Wombwell was driving round his estate with his head bailiff on another occasion when they saw an old woman gathering sticks in an area of the grounds which was forbidden to the villagers. Sir George ordered his man to go and see who she was but, as the bailiff approached, she slowly vanished, although she had been so clearly visible and so completely lifelike a few moments before.

One of the rooms of the Priory is very charming, yet seems to have a very uncanny atmosphere. Nearby is some oak panelling removed from the old grammar school, carved with the names of schoolboys long since gone - many of them being famous names in Yorkshire. The ghost is said to come from over the fireplace in one corner, and to bring with it a strong smell of burning. This part of the building was once destroyed by fire, and a lady was burnt to death.

On a mantel shelf there lies a Roman Catholic Book of Hours dating from the eighteenth century. It was said that if this prayer book were ever moved, whoever touched it would fall ill, and would not recover until someone else found it and replaced it in its accustomed position. This room is said to be the one in which punishments were meted out to any monk of the original Priory who disobeyed the Rule, and later it became known as the Justice Room where offenders were judged for such crimes as poaching and sheep stealing.

Just before the Priory was handed over to the King in 1539 a new room was being constructed in one of the upper storeys. This room was unfinished, and the Prior vowed that it would always remain incomplete. Any attempt to finish it met with disaster, so that eventually it was left as it was and used only for storage. Yet emerging from this room has been seen the figure of a man with silk breeches and a powdered wig, and a malevolent expression on his face. Doors, even when locked, have opened mysteriously, and the story is also told of a guest who became horribly aware of a misty, smoke-like emanation coming from a cupboard in the wall, and he was almost overcome by a terrifying sensation of strangling before he managed to force the thing back into the cupboard and lock the door!

Cawood

Old records often show strange stories of the past, and in the court records we find details of a murder case which was heard in York. The sentence was carried out, the culprit being hanged at White Cross Hill, Haxby Lane end, and his body later hung in chains near the scene of the crime. William Borwick, aged 45, was accused of the murder of his pregnant wife, having drowned her in a pond near Cawood Castle on April 14th, 1690. He told his wife's relations that she had gone to stay with an uncle near Selby, but suspicions were aroused when, according to "The Criminology of York Castle", "The apparition or spiritual appearance of the poor woman led to the discovery of the tragedy". Her ghost, dressed in a brown dress and a white hood, was seen near the pond, and her brother, Thomas Lofthouse, not believing William's story that he had sold his wife for five shillings, obtained a warrant for his arrest.

When he came to the scaffold, Borwick told the hangman that he hoped the rope was strong enough to bear him for, if it should break, he might fall to the ground and be crippled for life. The hangman politely assured him that he might venture upon it with perfect safety!

Fulford

Although no ghost has been reported at the site of this burial, one was obviously expected if we are to accept the evidence of another York trial. This concerned an officer of the garrison, Captain Bolton, who was sentenced in 1775 for the murder of his servant, Elizabeth Rambourne, at Bulmer on September 6th in the previous year, by strangling her and burying her body in his cellar. Whilst he was awaiting execution in York Castle he anticipated justice and hanged himself in his cell. He was buried at the three lane ends, near York Barracks, at ten o'clock at night, and a stake was driven through his body in the presence of the turnkeys of the Castle.

Raskelf

On Saturday, July 28th, 1623 a triple execution took place at the York Tyburn outside Micklegate Bar, and the bodies afterwards were hanged in chains near the scene of the crime. The culprits of this murder conspiracy were Ralph Raynard of the White House, near Easingwold, Mark Dunn of Huby and Mrs Fletcher, a lusty young woman from Thornton Bridge, according to the records. Although she had been "formerly too kind" with Raynard, she married a yeoman of good estate, one Fletcher of Raskelf. Marriage did not, however, end her relationship with Raynard, and eventually she conspired with him and with Mark Dunn of Huby to rid herself of her husband.

One May Day, as Dunn and Fletcher walked from Huby, Raynard and Mrs Fletcher lay in wait at Dawnay Bridge and drowned the unfortunate Fletcher. His body was then put in a sack, thoughtfully provided by his wife, and buried in Raynard's garden, mustard seed being sown to hide the grave. Mrs Fletcher and Raynard, explaining to neighbours that the missing husband had gone into hiding for fear of some writ being served upon him, were then able to continue "their wicked course of lust and drunkenness".

It would seem, however, that Fletcher had been somewhat suspicious of the activities of the three, and, some time before his death, had written to his sister:

"If I should be missing or suddenly in wanting be,
Ask Ralph Raynard, Mark Dunn, and my own wife for me."

Suspicion though was not strong enough to convict; stronger measures were obviously needed, and on the 7th July, when Raynard was saddling his horse in the stable before going to Topcliffe Fair, the spirit of Fletcher appeared, dressed and looking much as he had in life, and said,

"Oh Ralph, repent, for my vengeance is at hand".

After that the ghost appeared on many occasions, standing before Raynard with the same message, until, becoming sad and listless, he made confession to another person. His sister happened to overhear this and, fearful for her own life, she brought the information to Sir William Sheffield of Raskelf Park. All three were arrested, condemned and executed, their bodies hung in chains by the roadside not far from the White House where Raynard had lived, a spot subsequently given the name, Gibbet Hill.

Sutton-on-the-Forest

After one of the many television programmes about the ghosts of York, I received an interesting letter from a Mrs Dobson, now living in Scotland. She told me that as a child she lived in the vicarage of Sutton-on-the-Forest. (The old building has since been demolished and a modern one is in use.) Mrs Dobson says that although none of them ever saw anything, the whole family, including the dogs, were aware of a presence in parts of the house, and she will never forget the terror she felt. The strongest feeling was in the bathroom which was on the first floor, along a passage which formed one wall of the guest room. This room apparently was never used, and had a door which, although it led to the bathroom, was always kept locked. Another door led into the bathroom from the passage. Three steps led up from the bathroom to the locked door of the guest room. Often, anyone standing at the wash basin or sitting in the bath had an appalling feeling that someone, or something, was standing on the top step staring fixedly at them. Mrs Dobson says that not for anything would she have turned round to see what it was, but used instead to back out until she reached the other door, and then run along the passage and down the stairs.

The same feeling, though not quite so strong, was experienced in a passage which ran from the front of the house to the kitchen, lying directly below the one upstairs which was the bathroom corridor. Off the kitchen was a small room, used originally for hanging hams, keeping stores cool, etc. and the dreadful feeling was evident in there as well. Often as the dogs sat happily by the kitchen fire, the atmosphere changed, their hackles rose and they howled dreadfully, and neither they nor the cat would stay in the kitchen.

Mrs Dobson, having been brought up in the country, had no fear of the dark or anything else, but this feeling was one of absolute terror. Strangely enough she never mentioned this to her mother or brother until a conversation years later, after they had all left the vicarage, showed that they too had been aware of the atmosphere. Their mother then told them that the village people knew of the haunting, and would never go to the vicarage after dark, but no-one ever told them the story behind the haunt.

Rufforth

Another interesting letter came from a Mrs Armitage who spent some time at Rufforth when her husband was in the Air Force. One of the small upstairs rooms of the house in which she was living seems to have been the centre of a great deal of psychic activity. Guests, even those sceptical of psychic occurrences, didn't like sleeping there. Although the whole house had a strange atmosphere, full supernatural activity seemed to be confined to the room in question, and there were several instances connected with fire when it would seem that some force was at large. An oil stove overheated, and the whole room was blackened with smoke; baby clothes in a cupboard were burnt on another occasion, and her small son was found up there playing with matches, though nobody knew where he had got them from. A run of accidents, perhaps, except that Mrs Armitage saw a figure on several occasions standing at the door of that particular room. He was rather small, and dressed like a Puritan, but the most striking thing about him were his beautiful bright blue eyes. Being pregnant at the time, Mrs Armitage thought that she was imagining things but when, years later, she was telling her family about this, her son, who had only been about four at the time, said that he had also seen him. Was he, perhaps, there to protect the house? In that case, why, I wonder, was the ghost of a seventeenth century Puritan guarding the upper floor of a somewhat ordinary twentieth century house?

Scarborough

The east coast might seem rather far away for a York ghost to put in an appearance, but the story has often been recorded of the ghost in the pink dress. Lydia Bell was the daughter of a well known York confectioner, whose name can be found in the trade directories of the period. She had gone to stay at the Old Mansion House in St Nicholas Street, and here she met and was courted by a young officer, like many a girl before and since. Her father objected to this relationship, and forbade her to meet the officer again but, finding her somewhat rebellious, confined her to her room, and even, it is said, locked her in a cupboard. Yet, despite all these precautions, she managed to escape and went in search of the officer. Poor girl, she was not to return and her body was found on the beach the following morning. She had been strangled. The officer was immediately under suspicion, and evidence which brought him to trial was given against him by four men and a woman. He was, however, acquitted, though strangely enough three of the men who had denounced him came to untimely ends. One called Nicholson, who seemed to have known more about the case than he should have done, is said to have confessed to the murder on his deathbed, declaring that he had been driven to make his confession after seeing the ghost of Lydia Bell.

Since that time people living in the Georgian house have claimed to have seen Lydia, a slim, girlish figure wearing a pink dress - a crinoline some witnesses say, but, as the murder was committed in 1804, that particular style is somewhat unlikely - even for a fashionable and attractive ghost.

Back home again

I have often remarked how demolition, restoration or alterations to buildings seem, in some as yet unexplained way, to start ghostly activity. I received further confirmation of this in a clear and detailed letter regarding the Friends' Meeting House in Clifford Street, sadly but necessarily demolished very recently. After the old building had been declared structurally unsafe, it was the duty of the warden, Harry Buckle, to inspect the disused part of the premises at regular intervals. Late one afternoon, as Harry looked round the old Meeting House, now sad and empty, he saw quite clearly at the top of the tiered gallery the figure of a man dressed in traditional Quaker style, and wearing the familiar broad-brimmed hat. He looked down on Harry with an air of sadness, yet of sympathetic understanding, and there seemed to be between them a bond of Quaker silence before the figure slowly faded. Harry Buckle had lived there for many years, and was not at all a person who could be described as being ghostly-minded or over imaginative, but he was to see the figure again just before the old Meeting House was finally demolished. The psychic happenings began upstairs in the warden's flat. Doors opened without reason, and electrical faults occurred which the electrician could not explain. The behaviour of Toby, the black labrador, was even more curious. Toby was an easy going fellow, not given to nerves, and was never disturbed by any sudden noise. But recently he has acted very strangely, prowling the upstairs corridors with his hair bristling, and a hunted look in his eye.

My informant, to whom I am most grateful, wondered if this friendly spirit could be either William or Samuel Tuke who played such an important part in the early days of the Meeting House. Perhaps one of them just wanted to show that their interest in the old Meeting House was still very, very active after two hundred years.

The Shape of Ghosts to Come

My original intention in preparing this third edition was to add up to date information on continuing haunts and add new happenings over recent years. However, such has been the interest in our haunted city, as evidenced by world-wide coverage by authors, journalists and the many T.V. and radio broadcasts, that a great deal of material has accumulated. It is now planned therefore to assemble all this later information in a separate book, a sequel to what I have already published.

If any reader has any story of strange happenings in York and district which has not already been covered, I shall be most grateful to hear of it. I can give assurance that anything given to me will remain confidential until permission is given to use it, and will be treated in an unsensationalised, sympathetic and dignified manner.

John V. Mitchell